# *LADIES OF THE CHASE*

Published by
The Sportsman's Press in 1987



British Library Cataloguing in Publication Data

Buxton, Meriel
Ladies of the chase.
1. Women hunters—History
I. Title
799.2 SK21

ISBN 0-948253-14-2

Printed and bound in Great Britain by
BAS Printers Limited, Over Wallop, Stockbridge, Hampshire

# *LADIES OF THE CHASE*

**MERIEL BUXTON**

Foreword by
The Lord Paget
of Northampton, Q.C.

THE
SPORTSMAN'S
PRESS
*LONDON*

*To my Mother*
*and in memory of my Father*

# *CONTENTS*

# *FOREWORD*

## By The Lord Paget of Northampton, Q.C.

When I was a boy at the beginning of the century, girls were delicate creatures with soft round thighs; as the Irish put it, "beautiful things but no good in a fight". They did not ride side saddle by choice but of necessity. They could not ride astride because their thighs could not grip. Now all this nonsense is forgotten. Women ride as men ride and riding has become the only sport in which the sexes compete on genuinely equal terms. It has all happened in little more than half a century.

To take one particular branch, riding to hounds. When did women start riding to hounds? The first picture I have found is a Pollard (*c.* 1770) with the Royal Hunt in Windsor Park. She was right on their sterns, and so was George III, all 20-odd stone of him, but then a century elapses and it is a century that includes a whole school of hunting painters, Ferneley, Alken, Loraine Smith, Ward, Dean Wolstenholme and I cannot find a single woman participant. A progenitor of mine in about 1875 commissioned C.L. Ferneley to do pictures of the family at the meet of the Quorn and then coming home. According to the pictures, great-great-great-Aunt was the only lady at the meet and she had disappeared before the others turned for home.

I came across a copy of Bell's Life 1847 on Lady Foxhunters. "There is a wide difference between ladies hunting and ladies coming to the meet. They are as much in their place at the meet as they are out of it tearing across country."

Until the arrival of the new style side saddle so well described by Mrs. Buxton, this was surely true. On the old style saddle a woman could sit on a horse but she had no control. The new three- and later two-pommelled saddle was a great advance and exceptionally there were women who achieved a really beautiful balance. Mrs. Hopkins, a professional, show jumped side saddle at Olympia. True, show jumping in those days was not the television spectacular it was to become, but still, side saddle it was quite something. The new generation of sporting painters, Giles, Lionel Edwards, Simpson began to show women riding across country to hounds. There were not very many of them but they were now established as a growing minority in the hunting field.

At Cottesbrooke in the Pytchley country a certain gate on a canal bridge is still known as Lady Dalmeny's leap. With the Fernie in the early '20s Beryl van Raalte was better than most men. There were of course others but they were still rare.

A better side saddle was not the answer to women's need. The very pommels that made the riders' seat secure created the danger. As a horse rears or leaps the rider is pushed into the pommel. She cannot get off. She has no escape as the horse crashes down on her. As I write I can see the two fences where Mrs. Mason and ten years later my beautiful sister-in-law Baby Whitaker died because their pommels prevented them getting clear. If ever I was an M.F.H. again I would send side saddles home. They are for the meet, not for tearing across country. They are too dangerous.

Women's advance came when it was discovered that equitation depended on balance not grip and that a girl's balance was as good if not better than a man's.

Oddly enough it started with show jumping. Pat Smythe became the world's Number 1 show jumping personality for something like a decade, then even more strangely eventing, the toughest sport of all, gave us charming Lucinda Green, who has been followed by a number of other girls at least as good as the men.

Riding to hounds? Again I put a woman first: Lady Salisbury. For I think seven seasons we stabled our horses together in Leicestershire hunting with the Fernie, Quorn, Cottesmore plus occasional visits. She had the concentration of a terrier and wherever one was she was always in front. There was no point in looking anywhere else.

Mrs. Buxton is to be congratulated on the timing of her excellent book.

# *LIST OF ILLUSTRATIONS*

ACKNOWLEDGEMENTS

I would like to thank Her Majesty the Queen for her gracious permission to have photographs taken of side saddles within the Royal Mews, and to reproduce the illustrations numbered 3, 7 and 28.

Many people have helped me a great deal. In particular I would like to thank the following for the information and advice which they have given me and the time which they have spent on my behalf: Miss Effie Barker, The Hon. George Bathurst, Miss Carne-Williams, Lady Anne Cavendish Bentinck, Mrs. P.M. Borwick, Major A.S.C. Browne, Lady Dulverton, Mr. A.R.L. Escombe, The Countess of Feversham, Miss Mary Furness, Mrs. Gingell M.H., the late Mrs. Molly Gregson, Mrs. F.S. Hurndall-Waldron, Lady Lyell, Mr. A.S. Martyn M.F.H., Mrs. McKeever, Mr. T. Millar M.F.H., Captain T.D. Morgan, Mrs. R.P. Murphy M.F.H., Lord Paget, Count Guy de Pelet, Marjorie, Lady Pryse M.F.H., The Marchioness of Salisbury, Mrs. M.P.H. Simms, Sir Alexander Stanier, Sir John and Lady Thomson, Miss Thomson, Mr. Patrick Trimble, Lady Waechter M.F.H., Mr. and Mrs. R.G. Watson, Messrs. R.E. and G.B. Way, Mrs. N. Westendarp M.F.H., Mr. Harcourt Williams, Miss Elsie Wilson M.F.H. and Mrs. Rachel Woolett.

Finding suitable illustrations has been an enjoyable task because so many people have helped me with it. I would especially like to express my appreciation to Lord Yarborough for permission to use his portrait of Victoria, Countess of Yarborough on the front cover; to the Countess of Feversham and Count Guy de Pelet for the use of their pictures; to Mr. D.W. Fuller of Arthur Ackermann & Son Ltd., Mr. S. Ling of Fores Gallery Ltd., Mr.

Stephen Roberts of Frost and Reed Ltd. and Mr. I.R.D. Byfield of Richard Green Galleries, for all the very considerable help they have given me in selecting and obtaining pictures; to Colonel Sir John Miller for arranging for me to have photographs taken at the Royal Mews, to Mr. Green for all his help on the day and to Sir Anthony Rawlinson for actually taking the photographs; and finally to Mr. Jim Meads for his marvellous selection of photographs.

Despite extensive enquiries, I have been unable to trace the copyright owners of the picture of Skittles in the Bois de Boulogne or of Will Ogilvie's poem "The First Whip", and offer them my sincere apologies.

Finally, I owe a particular debt of gratitude to my long-suffering family: to my mother and brothers for their encouragement and help, to my children, who did not complain when their computer was turned into my word processor, but above all to my father who, before his death, gave me so much sound advice and constructive criticism and to my husband who has patiently and repeatedly read and commented upon endless drafts.

# CHAPTER ONE
# *MOSTLY ROYAL LADIES*

Ladies of the chase were worshipped as divine in the classical world. Diana or Artemis was the revered goddess of hunting, just as the Celts worshipped the goddess Epona. Young girls in ancient Greece won praise for the way they ran with hounds. Dido as well as Aeneas went hunting, and Xenophon wrote enthusiastically that "all men who have loved hunting have been good; and not men only, but those women also to whom the goddess has given this blessing", words which were to provide the title for that superb book on women and hunting, *To Whom the Goddess.*

Egyptians depicted themselves as accompanied by their womenfolk when they set out with boomerangs in boats in pursuit of wildfowl, or drove up beside the Nile in chariots hunting the wild animals of those parts. In China and Mongolia too hunting was not an exclusively male sport.

The Emperor Charlemagne was a keen hunting man who delighted in the company of his wife and daughters as well as of his sons in the hunting field. Whilst the hunting of the wild boar in his time took place within a confined space, in a walled park, Charlemagne's favourite sport was hunting the aurochs, or wild cattle of Europe. These were terrifyingly large animals which the Emperor would ride straight towards then kill with his drawn sword, in a manner perhaps more reminiscent of modern bull fighting than of hunting. On one occasion the terror shown by some visiting Persian ambassadors, who were invited to share the sport but panicked, resulted in Charlemagne being slightly hurt and his clothes torn. His only reaction was of amusement and a desire to share the joke with his wife Hildegarde, for she shared his enthusiasm for hunting. Six lofty, blonde, glamorous daughters also went with him, riding cross saddle and hunting at his side, to their father's pride and pleasure.

In England as well hunting was enjoyed by men and women alike, though the latter were always in the minority. This was partly because so much of women's time was taken up with child-bearing, which is perhaps why women in religious orders took a prominent part. Hunting, hawking and similar sports were not barred to them. Henry III sent a royal mandate to the Chief Forester of the County of Essex, bidding him "let the Reverend and Pious Ladye Mabel de Boxham" (Abbess of Barking) "have her dogs to chase hares and foxes."

Then there is the strange, shadowy figure of Juliana Berners, perhaps the first woman ever to write a book in the English language, if indeed she existed at all. The *Boke of St. Albans*, about hawking, hunting and fishing, was first printed in 1486. It has been suggested that Juliana Berners was the author, at least of the first two sections, that she was the daughter of Sir James Berners, who was beheaded in 1388, around the time of her birth, and that she became the Prioress of Sopwell nunnery near St. Albans. But evidence is lacking as she does not appear in the Berners family tree and there is a gap in the priory records between 1430 and 1480. The word "berner" means keeper of the hound, being derived from bran, part of the staple diet of hounds at the time. Whether this shows an hereditary interest in hunting, or whether she acquired the name through her enthusiasm for the sport rather than from her father remains a matter of conjecture. It has also been suggested that she was brought up at court, where she might well have become interested in hunting, for a number of 14th-century queens took an active part in the sport.

The most famous book on hunting of this time, the *Livre de Chasse* of Count Gaston de Foix, known as Gaston Phoebus, indicates that few women hunted at that time. However a plagiarised version was brought out in English by the Duke of York, son of Edward III and brother of John of Gaunt and the Black Prince, who was one of the very few Englishmen to die at the Battle of Agincourt, being suffocated in his armour. It was called *The Master of Game* and addresses itself to "all lords, ladies, gentlemen and women".

Edward II's wife Queen Isabella had her own pack of hounds, but they can have meant little to her, for, after taking them to Canterbury to hunt, she left them there for two years, which caused much irritation and inconvenience to the monks. Edward III's Queen Philippa had a fall out hunting and dislocated her shoulder. Then Richard II's adored Queen Anne of Bohemia was responsible for the introduction of a change which continued to affect the prospects of women in the hunting field for more than five hundred years. She introduced the side saddle to England.

Up to the end of the 14th century, women throughout the world are almost always depicted as riding astride. Anne of Bohemia introduced a side saddle, based on a pack saddle with a single pommel or horn in the front and a planchette or wooden plank as a foot rest along one side. The rider faced sideways with her two feet side by side on the planchette, almost as if she was in a chair without a back. It was customary though by no means invariable for women to sit on the nearside of the horse, for this enabled them to use the right hand to hang on to mane or pommel, or occasionally even to hold the reins. Soon the side saddle was in widespread use for decorative and formal occasions and for women who had no pretensions to being anything but passengers on the horse. At this time the cross saddle was still retained for those with more ambitions in the saddle, whether hunting or travelling. The 15th-century Ellesmere manuscript of the *Canterbury Tales*, for example, shows the nun and the prioress relaxing with their feet on planchettes, one on each side of the horse, whilst the more determined Wife of Bath rides astride. A variation on the planchette side saddle, designed to enable women to ride pillion behind men, was also popular. Indeed, this was the most suitable use for the planchette type side saddle, for the woman sitting on it and facing sideways had no prospect of being able to control her own horse.

The outstanding ladies of the chase in the 15th and 16th centuries were not English but European. Even in Italy there was no objection to the participation in the sport of the most fashionable ladies. Perhaps this was an extension of the Renaissance ideal of the complete man or woman, interested in everything. Those two cultured and elegant sisters Isabella and Beatrice d'Este, married respectively to the great Italian Renaissance princes Francesco Gonzaga of Mantua and Ludovico Sforza of Milan (whilst their brother was the fourth and last husband of Lucrezia Borgia, an experience he remarkably survived) were both highly intelligent and erudite. They were both great patrons of the arts, those attracted to Isabella's court including Leonardo da Vinci, Raphael, Titian and Castiglione. Yet both loved hunting, riding out immaculately dressed and covered with jewels. Beatrice wrote to her sister: "We are enjoying ourselves here very much, hunting every day." Certainly hunting at this time had a very different image from the late 17th- and early 18th-century English conception of the sport, when it was frequently considered, often unjustly, as the prerogative of drunken, boorish, semi-literate squires. This no doubt also accounts for the lack of prejudice in Renaissance times against the participation of women, so conspicuously reversed at the later date.

France in the 1460s and '70s was ruled with icy efficiency by King Louis XI, who crept spider-like about his palace, shabbily dressed, surrounded by guards, trusting no-one and imprisoning those who incurred his wrath for years on end in iron cages just large enough for a man to stand or lie down inside. Yet by subtle diplomacy he turned France from a weak, divided nation into a strong country with trade, agriculture and education all thriving. He would always support the middle classes against the aristocracy, and restricted the nobles' hunting in the interests of agriculture.

His daughter's sympathies in that case were probably with the aristocracy, for Anne of France, dame de Beaujeu, "loved hunting exceedingly". Yet in most other respects Anne closely resembled her father. When on his death she and her husband became Regents for her young brother Charles VIII she brought to her ruling of France much of her father's skill as well as many of his less attractive qualities: Louis' counsellor and biographer de Commynes soon found himself in an iron cage.

Despite the restrictions he placed on his nobles' hunting, Louis himself loved the sport and, according to de Commynes, "in the opinion of some people he understood it better than any other man of his generation". "He frequently returned tired out and nearly always angry with someone, for hunting is a sport which does not always go according to the plans of those in charge", as many a Master has discovered since.

His judgment in hunting matters was not infallible, for when an impoverished Breton squire made him a present of a white hound he showed little enthusiasm, for his own pack was dark coloured. The hound was first given to the Seneschal Gaston then put into the care of the Seneschal of Normandy, Jacques de Brézé, who entreated the king to give "the white hound from Barberie to the wisest ladie in his realm". The king, surprised, asked whom he meant.

"Your daughter, the Princess Anne of Beaujeu," he answered.

Louis snorted. "Say less foolish than the others," he retorted. "For there are no wise women in the world."

Louis was no doubt secretly pleased, and de Brézé, a great hunting man though violent when his passions were aroused (he suffered imprisonment for killing his wife and her lover when he found them in bed together), delivered the magnificent stallion hound Souillard to Anne.

Anne seems both to have been a good rider to hounds (de Brézé wrote a poem in appreciation of her skill across country) and a successful hound breeder. She fully appreciated "the beauty and goodnesse of this dogge" and used him as much as possible as a stallion hound. He provided the foundation stock for the Royal White Hounds of France, the best in Europe, noted for their steadiness, speed and resistance to rioting. This quality was not altogether appreciated at that time for a later hunting book records that before Souillard "white hounds were not much esteemed in France because they did not hunt all sorts of game, only deer." Soon his blood spread to England also. No hound before him had ever been so singled out and written about as an individual as Souillard became.

Anne of Beaujeu was as tough, hard and wily as her father had been before her. Whether she was hunting wolf or wild boar – and hunting wolves was as dangerous as almost any sport known – or governing France for her brother, she was as relentless and indefeasible as any man. During her Regency, she ensured that her brother the King married the young heiress Anne of Brittany, thus winning Britanny for France and the hatred of the fifteen-year-old princess for herself. Anne of Beaujeu yet had one quality which makes her less unattractive than her father: he never loved anyone or anything as she seems to have loved Souillard.

A close contemporary of Anne's was Mary of Burgundy, only child of Charles the Bold who was the lifelong enemy of Louis XI. Her father died when she was just nineteen and she was left Duchess of Burgundy and a much sought-after prize in the marriage market. Her sweeter, gentler nature made her a more attractive person than Anne. She found, with reason, that the political problems with which she had to grapple were awesome, especially when her tears and entreaties failed to save the lives of two of her father's old ministers from the hatred of the mob, but when she died just after her twenty-sixth birthday she was deeply loved by her people and had succeeded in bringing peace to her country.

Amongst the other parallels in their lives and despite the differences in their natures, Mary, like Anne, passionately loved hunting. She kept her favourite hound in her bedroom and has been described on horseback as "at ease, tireless and radiant with courage and gaiety". She was able to share this enthusiasm with the husband she eventually chose. Maximilian, the Holy Roman Emperor, was charming, attractive, brave and intelligent as well as extravagant, irresponsible and lacking in judgment. He also adored hunting, particularly chamois. It must have been particularly sad for him that his wife should have met her early death following a fall in the hunting field, although there is some doubt as to whether she was actually killed by the fall or died of a fever.

Appropriately those magnificent hunting tapestries designed by a pupil of Raphael, now in the Louvre and known as the Belle Chasse tapestries, were commissioned in memory of such parents by their daughter Margaret. Margaret was one of those fortunate children who seemed to inherit most of both her parents' good qualities without their failings. She had much of their charm and attractiveness but was a stronger, if less feminine, person than her mother with better judgment than her father. Perhaps this can be attributed to her education, which was largely overseen by that wise and forceful woman Anne of Beaujeu.

For Margaret was engaged as a small child, as was customary at the time, to the unattractive young son of King Louis XI of France, the future Charles VIII and brother of Anne. Margaret was therefore sent off to the French court to be educated there, which was a part of life for which Anne, keenly interested in the education of women, took responsibility. There she remained for eight years, until, as we have seen, Anne decided that it was more important for her brother to marry the Brittany heiress and Margaret was sent back to her father (a double slight, as her father had himself been planning to marry Anne of Brittany, with the scant regard to different generations paid in royal families at the time).

Marriageable daughters of Emperors were not left alone for long, and Margaret was soon dispatched to Spain to marry the charming young heir to the throne, Don Juan (brother of Henry VIII's Katherine of Aragon), whilst her handsome brother Philip was, less fortunately, married to another sister of Don Juan, Joanna the Mad. But just five months later Margaret's husband died, leaving her expecting his daughter, who also died not long afterwards.

However Margaret's time in Spain was brightened by her excellent relations with her mother-in-law, yet another powerful woman ruler of the time who loved hunting, Queen Isabella. But Margaret did not stay long in Spain, once again being fortunate in the husband chosen for her, Philibert Duke of Savoy, but unfortunate in that she had but three years with him before she was once more left a widow.

This time, though still only twenty-six, she did not remarry. Her brother too died young and a new career awaited her. Her brother left a young son, the future Emperor Charles V, who found himself heir to a massive inheritance including all Spain, Burgundy and the Holy Roman Empire. During his minority, Margaret was appointed Regent of the Netherlands, and even when Charles came of age he asked his aunt to continue her wise rule in that country. Not only was she Regent of the Netherlands, but she also took over the upbringing of her nephew Charles and three of his four sisters and performed both tasks with equal skill.

How she found time to rule a country, bring up a young adopted family, in a household filled with birds and animals of every description, and carry on an extensive correspondence with her father on affairs of state and matters of sport alike, as well as enjoying her own hunting, remains a mystery. However we are told that she could "undo a boar or brittle a stag with her own hands", and she required her ladies to be able to mount unaided, which probably indicates that she and they all rode astride.

It is remarkable how many of the great European rulers of the late 15th and 16th centuries were women, almost all of whom were noted also for their enthusiasm for hunting. Prominent amongst them is Margaret's mother-in-law, Isabella of Castile, whose marriage to Ferdinand of Aragon resulted in the unification of Spain. At the age of twelve she showed exceptional courage and determination by successfully resisting a marriage planned for her by her family, but she was already a girl with an independent mind. "Before she was ten she scorned the mule that etiquette ordained for women and children and kept her seat on a spirited horse. Days in the saddle made her hard, straight, resourceful, fearless, indifferent to fatigue, contemptuous of pain. . . . She became a skilful huntress, commencing with hares and deer, but later following the black wild boar, and on one occasion slaying a good-sized bear with her javelin."

Her intelligence, determination, energy and patriotism were in large measure responsible for the development of Spain into the great nation it was fast becoming. She encouraged art, music and learning, showed remarkable skill in picking those who served her and was much loved. She was a deeply religious woman, which led to a building up of the moral fibre of the whole country, but also meant that, with the best of intentions but, to modern eyes, appalling cruelty, she encouraged both the Inquisition and the persecution of Jews.

Her husband and many others were scornful when a young man appeared before them asking for backing for his seemingly wild dreams, but Isabella declared: "I will assume the undertaking for my own crown of Castile, and am ready to pawn my jewels to defray the expenses of it, if the funds in the treasury should be found inadequate." The suppliant's name was Christopher Columbus.

All these women managed to ride for long distances and must have had reasonably strong seats on their horses, which probably entailed facing forwards and not sideways. Yet this must have been extremely difficult to achieve at a time when there were no pommels for their legs to grip, merely a planchette on which to rest their feet. Some improvement was evidently called for, and was introduced later in the same century by another Queen.

That Queen was Catherine de Medici. She invented the second horn or pommel on the side saddle. Up to that time, as we have seen, there was a single horn in the middle of the saddle in front, which bears no relationship to either of the pommels on a modern side saddle and was apparently used rather as a handle. It was certainly not intended or designed for either of the legs to be supported by it. The weight of the legs fell on to the foot rest or planchette.

Catherine changed all this by adding a second horn below the first on the nearside of the saddle, the side where the legs were. This enabled the rider to hook her right leg (the front one) over the new pommel and wedge it between the two pommels, thus acquiring a much more secure seat than she had hitherto enjoyed. Yet astonishingly, as Lida Fleitmann Bloodgood points out in her book *The Saddle of Queens*, although Catherine spent a tremendous amount of time riding and hunting, this was not supposed to be her motive. According to the French historian Brantôme, she was concerned rather with showing off her legs, of which she was inordinately proud, by allowing her skirt thus to fall away from the front leg. Yet, as Brantôme's source for this information was one of the Queen's ladies-in-waiting, perhaps the lady-in-waiting was herself motivated by spite, or jealousy of the shape of the legs in question, and, if not a keen horsewoman herself, may have had no conception of the practical advantages of the new scheme.

At all events, this modification to the shape of the side saddle was the most important single change in riding for women from

Detail from "Early morning – a riding party setting out" by John Wootton. *c.* 1710. (*Courtesy of Arthur Ackermann & Son Ltd.*)

the time of the introduction of the side saddle until the invention in the middle of the 19th century of a third pommel, or leaping head, and the subsequent disappearance of the original first pommel.

Catherine de Medici came to France at the age of fourteen from her home in Italy as the bride of the Duke of Orleans, the future Henri II. Unfortunately for her, her husband was already infatuated with Diane de Poitiers, a passion which was to endure for the rest of his life. For ten long years she failed to produce the longed for baby which would stabilise her position, although she eventually became the mother of nine children. Bored perhaps, and possibly keen also to ingratiate herself with her father-in-law who had originally selected her for reasons of policy but who might eventually even sanction a divorce should he feel there was a risk of his line dying out, she begged to join the king on his hunting excursions. She finally persuaded him that she rode well enough to be worthy of inclusion and spent long hours in the hunting field, fanatically enthusiastic despite a number of unpleasant falls.

Perhaps originally also she hoped to win her husband's heart in the hunting field, for he passionately enjoyed the sport, but if this was in her mind she miscalculated, for her rival Diane de Poitiers excelled there too, and, brought up to hunt all her life, understood the finer points of the sport in a way Catherine the foreigner could never hope to emulate.

Yet Catherine is not a figure who elicits much sympathy. After the death of her husband and, a year later, of her eldest son, she became Regent successively on behalf of her next two sons, retaining her power for over twenty years. The *Encyclopaedia Britannica* describes her thus:

> "She had only one virtue, and that was her zeal for the interests of her children. . . . Like so many of the Italians of that time, who were almost destitute of a moral sense, she looked upon statesmanship in particular as a career in which finesse, lying and assassination were the most admirable, because the most effective, weapons."

Henri of Navarre, her opponent and son-in-law who eventually succeeded to the crown, was more charitable. He commented: "I ask you, what could one poor woman do, left by the death of her husband with five little children on her hands, and two families in France who were planning to seize the crown – ours and the Guises? Was she not forced to play strange parts, to deceive first one and then the other, in order to guard (as she has done) her sons, who have successively reigned by the wise conduct of that shrewd woman? I am suprised she never did worse."

Henri, as leader of the Huguenots, had more cause to hate her than anyone, for she chose to celebrate the occasion of his marriage to her daughter with the Massacre of St. Bartholomew, in which some eight thousand Huguenots died, and for which Catherine must accept responsibility.

With such a fearsome woman for a wife, it is small wonder that Henri II's devotion to Diane de Poitiers remained undiminished. Like Margaret of Austria, Diane was brought up in the "school" of Anne de Beaujeu, and is further convincing evidence of the success of Anne's policies of education. The reason she belonged to that elite group was that she was married at a young age to Louis de Brézé, some forty years her senior and son of the keeper of Souillard. Her husband and Anne herself between them taught her all there was to know about hunting and communicated their enthusiasm to her, without allowing her education in any other direction to be neglected.

When Francis I, Catherine's father-in-law, became King of France, his passion for hunting and his taste for a court peopled with beautiful women made Diane and her husband welcome courtiers. Yet Diane was close to thirty when the King's twelve-year-old son Henri first wore her black and white colours to take part in a tournament. A year later her husband, now in his seventies, died. She remained the dominant influence in Henri's life, as well as his mistress, for the twenty-nine years that remained to him.

Henri, like his father, adored hunting, but he had a very different nature from the flamboyant, extrovert Francis. Gentle and quiet, or "cold, haughty, melancholy and dull" depending on the point of view, he was a superb horseman but a shy and retiring man. Diane gave him the confidence he lacked. A contemporary wrote of her: "No lady was ever better on horseback . . . and she was very lovely of face and figure. . . . She spoke Italian, Spanish etc."

Diane also succeeded in turning her Château d'Anet into an

earthly paradise for Henri. It was described as "*un véritable rendezvous de chasse*" with its kennels, mews and cages but it was also superbly decorated with an outstanding library, altogether a fitting setting for the Duchess of Valentinois, as Henri created her. She helped her King to make Chenonceaux equally beautiful and he needed little encouragement to treat her as his queen and to pour money and estates on her, thus inadvertently creating for her many bitter and jealous enemies. When Henri was accidentally killed in a tournament, Diane retired to her estates.

Whilst these women were especially noted for their love of hunting, most of those at court, men and women alike, took an active part in the sport. Mary Queen of Scots for instance, whose first husband was the short-lived eldest son of Catherine de Medici, had a nasty fall which the English ambassador in Paris described in detail in his report home, telling how she was lucky not to be ridden over, concluding that "she feleth no incommodite by her fall; and yet she hath determined to chaunge that kind of excercise." After the death of Henri IV (Henri of Navarre) his widow, Marie de Medici, kept the Royal Hunt going in the same style as had her husband, going out with a number of ladies on horses, and as many as four or five hundred gentlemen, a depress-

"Family Hunting Party" by Judith Lewis. 1755/6. (*Courtesy of Arthur Ackermann & Son Ltd.*)

ingly large field. Her erstwhile rival, Henri's mistress Gabrielle d'Estrées, always wore green and, more remarkably, rode astride.

Stag hunting, coursing and falconry were all popular in sixteenth-century England, and Queen Elizabeth was considered to be very keen on the sport. She and Leicester behaved most unsportingly on a visit to Berkeley Castle, when, in the absence of the owner, they killed twenty-seven of his stags. Lord Berkeley on his return was so angry that he came close to destroying his park and giving up keeping deer at all. Even a mere three years before her death she was described as being "excellently disposed to hunting, for every second day she is on horseback and continues the sport long". But English hunting at this time was inferior to European, and in particular French, hunting, for it was almost entirely confined to enclosed parks. The French ambassador wrote home unimpressed:

> "The English are not as skilled in taking the stag as they are in marine matters. . . . They took me to a great park full of fallow deer, where I mounted a Sardinian horse, richly caparisoned, and in company of forty or fifty lords and gentlemen we hunted and killed fifteen or twenty beasts."

Often the deer would be hunted round such an enclosed area by greyhounds, whilst the Queen and her friends shot at them with cross bows from specially constructed pavilions. Whilst, in fairness to Elizabeth, she was noted as an excellent shot who would usually kill cleanly, the system resulted in mass slaughter and many wounded beasts, as well as being too artificial to offer any of the true pleasures of hunting.

In such undesirable circumstances, the misadventure which befell Queen Anne of Denmark, wife of James I, is understandable. A Mr. Chamberlain in 1613 tells what happened: "Queen Anne of Denmark shooting at a buck killed instead one of the king's most principal and special hounds, called 'Jewel'. On which the King stormed exceedingly, but after he knew who did it was soon pacified and with much kindness wished her not to be troubled with it and next day gave her a magnificent diamond worth two thousand pounds in remembrance of his poor dead dog."

The same Queen was pictured at Hampton Court with a horse standing beside her and hounds all round her feet. She and her son sent twenty couple of beagles as a present to the young French

"Anne of Denmark" by Paul van Somer. (*Reproduced by Gracious Permission of Her Majesty the Queen.*)

king, Louis XIII.

Although in the 17th century the great majority of women rode side saddle, there were exceptions, as we have seen in the case of Gabrielle d'Estrées. Sometimes even the onlookers were uncertain as to which style was being adopted. Queen Christina of Sweden was generally believed to have made her ceremonial entry into Rome in 1655 riding cross saddle, an illusion created by her strong, straight, forward-facing seat. A year later she was described as entering Paris "clad from head to foot in scarlet, and had black plumes in her hat. She rode astride on a magnificent white horse, richly caparisoned with gold and silver – a cane in her hand and pistols slung from her saddle bow." Whether this was the result of a similar mistake or whether she in fact used both saddles is not clear.

A century later royal ladies by no means inevitably rode side saddle. Catherine the Great of Russia not only rode astride herself but ensured that her ladies did likewise. Marie Antoinette, when she became Queen, did adopt a side saddle, but in her days as wife of the Dauphin not only rode cross saddle but combined her exotically feathered hat and "profusion of gold lace" with breeches and boots but no skirt, dress regarded at the time as more appropriate for a man than a lady.

So women throughout the western world were enjoying their hunting on more or less equal terms with the men during the 15th, 16th and 17th centuries. Most of those of whom we hear were royal, not because they were the only women to hunt but because only their activities were considered worthy of comment by the writers of the time. For much of this time, the hunting in Europe was superior to that in England, though this was a position which was fast changing. During this time, the most important development in riding for women was made by a woman, even though Catherine de Medici is not an inspiring example of her sex. However the honour of the ladies of the chase was upheld in fine spirit by such women as Anne of Beaujeu, Margaret of Austria and Diane de Poitiers.

# CHAPTER TWO

# *SOME EARLY LADY MASTERS*

At the start of the 18th century, in Queen Anne's time, whilst considerably fewer women than men hunted, no social stigma was attached to female participation. The Queen herself, always a sporting lady, was a great enthusiast, with hunting coming second only to racing for her. Often too ill to ride herself, she established hounds at Ascot and took much trouble with the country, having view rides cut and bogs drained. She would often drive herself to hounds in a light vehicle known as a calash, driving "furiously like Jehu" and, according to Jonathan Swift, once covered forty-five miles after a stag before dinner.

Whilst the royal family, the court and a few of the most aristocratic families hunted deer, the country gentlemen hunted the hare. At least one lady at this time hunted her own pack of harriers. Lady Harley was born, in 1696, Henrietta Cavendish-Holles, daughter of the Duke of Newcastle and heiress to an enormous fortune. Her maternal grandfather, also a Duke of Newcastle, was the outstanding horseman of his generation.

In 1713 Henrietta married Edward Harley, subsequently second Earl of Oxford, and son of Robert Harley, leading statesman of the time, whose rift with his rival Bolingbroke eventually led to the downfall of both. In 1716, when Lady Harley was portrayed by Wootton resplendent in scarlet habit with gold tassels, her father-in-law was a prisoner in the Tower of London.

Lady Harley, who became Countess of Oxford on the death

"The Countess of Oxford" by John Wootton. (*Private collection. Photograph by Layland Ross.*)

of the old statesman in 1724, had just one daughter, Margaret, who married the second Duke of Portland. The Countess of Oxford thus numbers amongst her descendants not only a grandson who became Prime Minister but many great sporting men and women, including successive Dukes of Portland, Lord Henry Bentinck and Lord George Bentinck.

In later life, Lady Oxford was a figure of eminent, almost stultifying, respectability. She was also on excellent terms with the family into which she had married, which was one of exceptional culture and erudition (the Harleian Library formed the nucleus of the British Museum) with little sympathy for sporting interests. Her sister-in-law wrote of an eight-year-old nephew: "I hope he will be brought to delight in his Book and that Westminster School will put Dogs and Horses out of his head which already he begins to despise."

Others came to hunting later in life. Lady Mary Wortley Montague, unconventional, much-travelled and highly intellectual, had little use for hunting in her younger days but later became enthusiastic. She wrote to her sister: "I pass many hours on horseback and, I'll assure you, ride stag hunting, which I know you'll stare to hear of. I have arrived at vast courage and skill in that way, and I am well pleased with it as with the acquisition of a new sense."

The appearance of women in the hunting field caused none of the surprise of a century later. Pope wrote in 1717 of meeting the Prince of Wales "with all his maids of honour on horseback coming from hunting." Pope added that some of Queen Anne's maids of honour hunted only because the Queen made them, and he:

> ". . . agreed that to eat Westphalia ham in a morning, ride over hedges and ditches on borrowed hacks, come home in the heat of the day with a fever, and what is a hundred times worse a red mark in the forehead from an uneasy hat; all this may qualify them to make excellent wives for fox-hunters and bear abundance of ruddy complexioned children but is highly disagreeable to many!"

A writer in *The Spectator* was even more scathing:

> "I have very frequently the opportunity of seeing a rural Andromache, who came up to town last winter, and is one of the greatest fox-hunters in the country; she talks of hounds and horses and makes nothing of leaping over a six bar gate. If a man tells her a waggish story, she gives him a push with her hand in jest, and calls him an impudent dog; and, if her servant neglect his business, threatens to kick him out of the house; I have heard her in her wrath call a substantial tradesman a lousie cur."

Such women, then and now, give their sport a bad name. But the presence of women out hunting was not generally frowned on. A painting of a hunting scene in 1723 featuring George I and many important political and diplomatic figures includes the wife of the Secretary of State, her presence clearly regarded as diplomatically desirable. Princess Amelia, daughter of King George II, enjoyed hunting with the staghounds, despite an

"The Princess Amelia accompanied by her groom Spurrier" by James Seymour *c.* 1740. (*Courtesy of Arthur Ackermann & Son Ltd.*)

unpleasant fall when her petticoat was caught on the pommels of the saddle causing her to be dragged for some two hundred yards.

The narrator in Sir Walter Scott's *Rob Roy* describes his first sight, in 1715, of the heroine Die Vernon thus:

> "She wore, what was then somewhat unusual, a coat, vest and hat, resembling those of a man, which fashion has since called a riding habit. The mode had been introduced while I was in France and was perfectly new to me. Her long, black hair

streamed on the breeze, having in the hurry of the chase escaped from the ribbon which bound it. . . . I had, therefore, a full view of her uncommonly fine face and person, to which an inexpressible charm was added by the wild gaiety of the scene, and the romance of her singular dress and unexpected appearance."

Enthusiasm is coloured with surprise at the style of dress rather than the presence in the hunting field.

Another fictional heroine who figures prominently in the hunting field appears in *Tom Jones*, which is set in Somerset in the 1740s. Squire Western encouraged his daughter to hunt, spending sixty guineas on a five-year-old sorrel mare for her. Like Die Vernon's family, Squire Western personifies many of the less attractive features often attributed to hunting men, particularly at this period. They are portrayed as drunken, boorish squires, violent in language and often behaviour, lacking any polish, erudition or finer feelings. If such men were indeed typical, it is the more remarkable that female participation was not considered the scandalous eccentricity of a century later.

During the course of the 18th century, fox hunting gradually took over from hare hunting until in 1792 "fox hunting is now considered as the only chase in England worthy of the taste or attention of a highbred sportsman." A number of modern packs of foxhounds date their origins to around the middle of this century.

The first Master of the Quorn, Thomas Boothby, is believed to have held office from 1698 to 1753. He had a mistress, Catherine Holmes, who probably also rode to hounds. In his will, he bequeathed to her "the horse she usually rides, with the bridle and saddle".

She had earlier been the unwitting cause of much local merriment. The parson, an enormously fat man whose name was Pike, revealed to Boothby's wife that he kept a mistress at Groby Pool House. Boothby, vowing vengeance, persuaded the parson to meet him at the pool and pushed him into the water. The reverend gentleman was not a swimmer; he was eventually brought to land almost lifeless, dragged in by his assailant in a net. For years afterwards the villagers recalled the day an eighteen-stone pike was taken out of their pool.

The same pool was chosen by Loraine Smith for his light-

"A Hunting Scene at Groby Pool" by C. Loraine Smith. 1822. The chimney sweep follows Lady Graham on the right in the foreground. (*Courtesy of Fores Gallery Ltd.*)

hearted hunting scene featuring Lady Graham and a chimney sweep with whom she formed a notorious liaison. Whilst there is little doubt that the sweep never in fact appeared on the hunting field, the artist could not resist including him.

The first Master of the Holderness, William Draper, held office from 1726 to 1746. A generous man though not a rich one, on seven hundred pounds a year he succeeded in dressing and mounting his family of eleven sons and three daughters. One daughter in particular, Diana, made a great name for herself when she whipped-in to her father, and was renowned for her holloa and for her reckless riding.

Eighteenth-century foxhunting was a very different proposition from that of the 20th century. It was conducted at quite a different pace. Hounds were of the old Southern type, very slow with a great cry. Days were long and started early, two factors which seem to have discouraged many women from taking part. A run with Sir Roger de Coverley's hounds is recorded in which he killed his fox after fifteen hours' riding, having passed through half a dozen counties, killed two horses and lost "above half his dogs".

As the country had not then been enclosed, the only fences normally encountered were park fences or gates, ditches and sometimes a hedge. The land was undrained and very heavy and neither hounds nor horses, nor indeed the fox, considered it necessary frequently to go faster than a trot. Such fences as were jumped were never jumped galloping on, and what was described as a "flying leap" was both rare and unnecessary. Typical of an outstanding hunt was that enjoyed by the Grafton in 1745 : sixty miles in twelve hours. As no-one then had second horses and horses were all unclipped, unnecessary galloping about would have been most unwise by anyone anxious to see the end of such a hunt or concerned with his horse's welfare.

Even at this pace, the sport had risks for the rider. King George III, with exceptional honesty, avowed: "I love hunting, but I fear leaping. A King and the father of a family should not ride bold." His concern extended to ladies: in 1793 a Mr. Griffin Wilson drove his lady in a phaeton after the hounds so daringly that the King, irritated, asked whether he thought he had driven fairly or not. When Mr. Wilson made no reply, the King told him that, whatever right a gentleman had to his own neck, he had none to hazard a lady's. We are not told whether the lady in question appreciated the royal concern or had found the hunt as exciting as had her escort.

Galloping on over fences was only feasible for men because a flat hunting saddle had already been introduced. The alteration in design preceded the need for it in the hunting field. Women were less fortunate. The side saddle of the time had two pommels as does a modern side saddle. They were however in different positions from the modern pommels. The rider normally sits on the left or nearside of the horse. On the modern side saddle the right leg is supported from underneath by the higher pommel. The lower pommel, or leaping head, comes just above the left leg enabling the woman to obtain a purchase against it with her left thigh. Thus, and only thus, can she grip sufficiently to enable her to gallop on and jump fences at speed without using a hand to hold on to the back of the saddle. The 18th-century saddle also had two pommels, but one was below and the other above her right leg. There was no leaping head. It is more remarkable in these circumstances that a few women succeeded in managing the standing jumps required at the time than that they were subsequently unable to cope with the transition to "flying leaps".

The obvious modern solution, for women to ride cross saddle, was inconceivable to 18th-century ladies. Two young ladies from Bury in Suffolk had the temerity to appear astride in "smart doeskins, great coats and flapped beaver hats". They had been educated abroad. Their appearance occasioned "many sarcasms". Women in breeches were considered indecent. Habits were more becoming: George Sand's appearance in breeches in the next century caused her to be described as having the biggest bottom in France. How much more elegant were the royal and court ladies who hunted with the buckhounds in the 1770s in their blue habits faced and turned up with red, and white beaver hats with black feathers.

By Regency times skirts, veils and the numerous petticoats underneath had become long, flimsy and trailing. They were not only impractical but dangerous, as will be seen in the next chapter. This was another change for the worse for women who wished to take an active part in the hunting field. In the picture of Lady Harley in 1716, whilst her habit is magnificently trimmed and of exotic material, the skirt is cut straight at the bottom: the pointed, trailing garment was not then inevitable as it subsequently became.

A few ladies still continued to come out with hounds at this time. Juliana Ludford, of Ansley Hall in Warwickshire, was hunting regularly in the 1770s and 1780s with Lord Donegall's, Mr. Kinnersley's and Lord Belfast's hounds. She describes a day in 1777 thus:

> "In October 1777 I went from Fisherwick Hall with Lord Donegall in his postchaise a fox-hunting. The hounds met at Polesworth, where we got on horseback, and after waiting some time for the fog to clear, went and drew the woods on the common and Bagley Woods, where we found a fox and ran him away to Birch Coppice, and from thence towards Polesworth, then back again through Birch Coppice where he went to ground. Lord Donegall and myself were thrown out for a considerable while and rode I suppose at least three times round the hounds after the fox went to ground . . . we saw one of the whippers-in who had been to Atherstone for the terriers who told us where the hounds were and we then went to them

and found them digging for the fox which at length they dug out and killed. Timothy brought back a foot. We then went to Atherstone with the hounds, dined there and then went back, to Fisherwick."

Lady Jersey and Lady Conyngham were amongst those hunting with the Prince of Wales in the 1790s. Whilst a few women truly rode to hounds, many more put in an elegant appearance at the meet then rode quietly about accompanied by a groom.

By the start of the 19th century ladies of the court no longer rode out with hounds socially. Almost all women who hunted were either wives or daughters of Masters of Hounds, or else they were women who were brazenly aware that they had no reputation to lose.

Lady Craven was amongst those able to hunt with her husband's hounds. Successive Earls of Craven were Masters of the Craven Hounds from 1739 to 1804. A contemporary wrote: "As I recollect, Lady Craven, upon Pastime, never shrank from either fence or timber." No doubt the "flying leap" had not yet been adopted in Craven country. Even so it cannot have been easy to ride a horse into a fence seated on a saddle on which one had no means of gripping.

Mrs. Thornton in 1804 went beyond even the hunting field. An argument between her and her brother-in-law over the respective merits of their horses led to a match race between the two. The lady was made favourite but, despite putting up an impressive performance and winning much admiration for her horsemanship as well as her looks and turn-out, she was just beaten.

The most infamous of the Regency women who appeared in the hunting field was Lady Lade. An elegant portrait of her by Stubbs was commissiond by the Prince of Wales, who was amongst her admirers. Laetitia Lade did not start life in such exalted circles. Of gypsy birth and a cook by trade, one of her earliest lovers was a notorious and popular highwayman known as "Sixteen String Jack", who was eventually hanged in the '70s. Letty attracted much attention at his execution and never looked back.

She eventually married Sir John Lade. Finest whip of all the Regency rakes and professional coachmen too – he taught the Prince of Wales to drive – he exceeded them also in habits and

"Laetitia, Lady Lade" by Stubbs. (*Reproduced by Gracious Permission of Her Majesty the Queen.*)

language. His wife alone was a match for him on every count.

Well able to handle a coach and eight, she was equally conspicuous in the hunting field. *The Sporting Magazine* speaks of her as always being well up, and after a good run in October 1796 she was declared to be the first horsewoman in the kingdom. Three years later she once more excelled in the run of the season, a hunt lasting two hours and forty minutes. "Lady Lade kept up the whole time – her fleet courser never failed."

Lady Lade was as well known for her foul language as for her skills at riding and driving. It has been suggested that she was the inspiration for Surtees' character Lucy Glitters. If so, the author softened and toned down his model remarkably to produce his wild but attractive heroine. A truer picture of Lady Lade is probably that painted by Sir Arthur Conan Doyle in his historical novel about that time, *Rodney Stone*. She is there portrayed as taking part with her husband in a driving match against the fictional hero. When the Lades face defeat, her Ladyship, not the more sporting Sir John, pulls her leader across her opponent's wheel on a narrow bridge, injuring her own horse and intending to put the other vehicle over the side into the deep gully below.

One who might have rivalled Lady Lade in toughness and in the way she rode across a country, although socially she moved in less exalted circles, was Phoebe Higgs, mistress of Squire George Forester. Squire Forester of Willey Hall in Shropshire is amongst the legendary figures of early hunting, his name coupled with that of his celebrated whipper-in Tom Moody. Squire Forester was hunting hounds by 1773 and died in 1811. His country comprised much of the modern Wheatland country. Rising at first light, they had some exceptional hunts. One well-known fox was nicknamed Old Tinker and the Squire had sworn to "follow the devil this time to Hell's doors". Hounds hunted that fox for over fifty miles before Forester's horse, now ridden by Moody, fell dead. Hounds also had had more than enough, but Old Tinker's triumph was short-lived: he was found dead in a ditch a few days later. It is said to be the pace which kills, but the enormous distances of late 18th-century hunting took a terrible toll of hounds and horses as well as foxes.

Squire Forester and Tom Moody lived a wild, drunken life: perhaps the tales of their exploits grew as the port bottle emptied. They epitomised much of the best as well of the worst of hunting of the time. The drunken debauchery and cruelty were matched by courage and determination. What is more remarkable is that Forester found a woman willing to share his days as well as his nights. Phoebe Higgs was a great horsewoman with an unshakeable nerve. She would jump places everyone else thought unjumpable, daring Forester and Moody to follow her. A kind-hearted woman, she spent her free days visiting the poor, but could also look after herself. Deciding that her allowance was inadequate, she took a loaded pistol, prepared to shoot the Squire if he did not accede to her demands.

In 1775 the first woman took office as Master of Foxhounds. The first Marchioness of Salisbury was unlikely to be deterred by other people's opinions: much of her life was spent in doing things which other people considered shocking. A heavy gambler, she gave the Rector little support. She first heard the story of Adam and Eve at a service at Hatfield and reacted indignantly to Adam's churlish behaviour in blaming his wife: "Shabby fellow indeed!" she exclaimed aloud. She entertained on a truly magnificent scale and her whole way of life was ostentatious and domineering. She dressed exotically and liked to float down the river in a barge attended by a dozen liveried menservants, or drive round the estate throwing golden guineas to the tenants. Her language could be coarse, her manner imperious. After the music had started at a Handel festival in Westminster Abbey attended by the king, loud hammering was heard coming from Lady Salisbury's box: she had decided to have a partition moved.

"The Countess of Salisbury". From *To Whom the Goddess* by Lady Diana Shedden and Lady Apsley (*Reproduced by kind permission of the Hon. George Bathurst.*)

Despite her failings, she was an enthusiast and a sportswoman. When her husband's interest in hunting waned, she took on the Mastership and established the Hatfield Hunt. Her hounds were dwarf foxhounds, noted for their steadiness and fine noses. Fields of forty to eighty hunted, many gentlemen staying at Hatfield, the remainder consisting of farmers and horse dealers.

The Master went well across the country. In March 1795, a contemporary wrote: "Out of a field of fourscore her ladyship soon gave honest Daniel the go-by; pressed Mr. Hale neck and neck, soon blowed the whipper-in, and continued indeed, throughout the whole of the chase, to be nearest the brush."

Lady Salisbury devised a uniform for herself of a sky blue habit with black velvet collar and a jockey cap. Besides hunting, her sporting interests included driving a four-in-hand and archery, on which latter subject she wrote in the first number of *The Sporting Magazine*.

Lady Salisbury remained Master until she was near seventy in 1819, and continued hunting after that. Eventually she could only stay on a horse if strapped to the saddle and was so blind that she required a pad groom not just to pilot her but to take her horse on a leading rein. When they reached a fence, the groom gave a warning shout: "Damn you, my Lady, jump!" and together they jumped. Farcical and undignified though it was to others, this performance demanded considerable courage and determination.

Whilst her acquaintance laughed and nicknamed her Old Sal or Old Sarum, she was a trial to her family, being supremely selfish and demanding as well as hopelessly extravagant. The diarist Creevey describes her thus:

> "It is impossible to do justice to the antiquity of her face. If, as alleged, she is only seventy-four years old, it is the most cracked, or rather furrowed, piece of mosaic you ever saw; but her dress, in the colours of it at least, is absolutely infantine." [He describes her white muslin dress and bright lilac and yellow ribbons. Two years later he saw her again:]
>
> "Sall being the only one who mounted her horse like an arrow from the hand of her groom, the horse too being an uncommonly high one, milk white, dressed in a net, and a present (as she informed me) from her Son Salisbury" [father of the Prime Minister] "who had given two hundred guineas for it . . . Tho' I did not discover any of the talent Sefton gives her credit for, her opinions upon different matters were very

amusing."

Her death was a terrible one. She was writing in her room at Hatfield when the feathers in her hair probably caught fire in the candle. With a high wind blowing, the fire soon destroyed Lady Salisbury herself and the whole of the west wing. Only a change in the wind enabled the rest of Hatfield to be saved. At first the family jewels also were thought to have been burnt: later it became clear that these had long been sold and paste copies substituted.

By the end of the 18th century, women's position in the hunting world should have been much stronger than at the start of that century. A few women had displayed remarkable skill and courage in riding across a country. Large numbers had come out with hounds without incurring more than passing criticism. One had become a Master of Foxhounds and held that position with great success for forty-four seasons.

Yet the number of women who would ride to hounds in the first sixty years of the 19th century could almost be counted on the fingers of one hand. The revolution in hunting which had already started in Leicestershire under Hugo Meynell soon spread over all England. It served to make the handicaps under which women already struggled intolerable. The social climate too was changing. The excesses of Regency England, when the very wildness of Lady Lade made her a court favourite, were fast giving way to the equally excessive restrictions of the Victorian age, when women's activities were confined within the walls of home.

# CHAPTER THREE
# *THAT SPITTERCOCKATION PACE*

"What fun we should have if it were not for these damned hounds!" remarked Lord Alvanley early in the 19th century. The thought has been echoed, generally with less candour, a thousand times since by those who hunt to ride. Before Hugo Meynell's Mastership of what are now the Quorn Hounds it would have made no sense at all. For foxhunting in its modern form originated in Leicestershire during Meynell's Mastership which lasted from 1753 to 1800, the ripples gradually spreading to the rest of Britain.

Meynell was an intelligent, educated man who applied his capable brain to the breeding of the foxhound, as indeed a number of his contemporaries were doing elsewhere in England: Peter Beckford in the West, the Earl of Yarborough at Brocklesby and others. He was no doubt influenced by his near neighbour Robert Bakewell's celebrated work on the breeding of farm animals. Certainly by 1800 he had a high class pack of hounds which, so far from walking a fox to death as his predecessor Thomas Boothby's hounds had done, excelled in the two qualities Meynell rated most highly: they had fine noses and were stout runners.

By the time he had transformed his hounds in this way, Hugo Meynell had outgrown the wild days of his youth, when he had been described as the "worst sportsman and wildest huntsman" ever seen out with hounds. It was left to the younger generation to appreciate the potential of a pack of hounds which could run on so fast. Amongst those who did so and came to Leicestershire especially to hunt was William Childe of Kinlet in Shropshire, nicknamed the Flying Childe. He was probably the first to gallop on over his fences, "riding up to the hounds and flying the fences as they came". Mr. Meynell was horrified, but it was too late: soon all the young men were doing the same thing. About the time Meynell retired, Childe returned to his native county to spread the new system there.

A third factor combined with the improvement in hound breeding and the newly felt desire to gallop on over fences (and consequent improvement in the calibre of horse) to make hunting the sport it has remained. Before the middle of the 18th century the country was largely unfenced, and even by the end of Hugo Meynell's regime was only slowly becoming enclosed. During the reign of George III (1760–1820) some 3,500 Enclosure Acts were passed, compared with a total before that of between 200 and 250, although the actual erecting of fences might be spread over a considerable period of time after the date of the Act for a particular parish. The fences put up at this time in Leicestershire, often designed to keep in heavy bullocks, could be formidable. The foundations of the fences of the future would be laid with a ditch and newly planted quickthorn hedge. Then the immature hedge would need the protection of an ox rail (in place of the barbed wire backfences of today). Those places where an ox rail was put up on each side were known as double oxers.

These new developments in the sport were most exciting for hunting men. For women they were disastrous, not through any real or imagined deficiencies in women's strength, nerve or horsemanship, but for one practical reason. It was almost, though not quite, impossible to gallop on and jump fences at speed on the side saddles then available, and no woman seems to have considered riding astride. Before the introduction of what Meynell termed "that spittercockation pace", it was possible, if difficult, for women to jump such fences as they encountered, probably by using one hand to grasp the back of the saddle and steady themselves, as Lady Lade, the Countess of Salisbury and others had proved. Galloping on over country divided into twenty- or thirty-acre enclosures, jumping fences frequently and fast, made this an extremely hazardous undertaking, and a horse, to compete on equal terms with the men's, would generally require both hands on the reins coming into its fences. Thus for the next half century, until the introduction of the third pommel or leaping head on the saddle, women in the hunting field, other than a decorative sprinkling at the meet, became so scarce as to be almost unknown. Early in the 19th century the two Loraine Smith girls from Enderby, sisters of the artist, their mother and a Miss Stone from

"An elegant Equestrienne on a grey" by Alfred de Dreux (1810–1860). Most impractical for riding across a country. (*Courtesy of Frost and Reed.*)

Blisworth, were said to be the only ladies hunting in Leicestershire. The two sisters rode in scarlet bodices and grey skirts.

For the side saddle, despite modifications in details and in the materials of which it was made, was substantially the same in 1800 as when Catherine de Medici invented the second horn more than two hundred years earlier. Leather, rather than brocade or velvet, was now the basic material, but before the invention of the leaping head, described in the next chapter, there was no possibility of getting sufficient purchase to have a strong independent seat when jumping.

Clothes also were most impractical for riding across a country. Skirts were long, full and flowing, both frightening and potentially dangerous for the horse. The hat, so far from affording any protection to the head, tended to be large and exotic, preferably bedizened with an elaborate plume or feather, or occasionally with an immense brim which must have caught every gust of wind. Everything about the dress of the day emphasized the exotic and fluffy, muslin being the most fashionable material, quite the reverse of the smooth, neat, inconspicuous line aimed at by all the smartest women riders of the last hundred years. Hair could be full, long and curly, with no attempt made to control it, veils when worn were as flowing as the skirt, and the neck was adorned with as much lace as possible.

As late as the 1840s and '50s, when Mrs. Poulett Somerset was hunting, she always wore a large brown straw hat with a drooping ostrich feather and flowing veil. Yet, being the daughter of the renowned hard-riding eccentric John Mytton and herself noted as one of the hardest women to hounds in her day, she was hardly the sort of woman to go in for unnecessary and inconvenient frippery.

Not only the outside appearance was impractical. No lady early in the 19th century considered wearing breeches under her skirt. As the vast majority of women rode simply as a means of transport, they wore clothes appropriate to the function to which they were travelling rather than special riding clothes. Those with more ambitions in the saddle perhaps modified their outer garments a little, but at this stage did no such thing for what was underneath, which must have made riding at all extremely uncomfortable. Thus the long, trailing and often numerous skirts were not merely decorative but essential in the interests of decency, which required the lady's ankles to remain covered at all times, despite all attempts by the wind to disturb the perfect symmetry of the flowing garment. Lapses were the more conspicuous in that the skirt covered voluminous petticoats. As late as 1860 a book urging that "all superfluity of underclothing should be dispensed with," still added "the error of extremes into which some ladies run by the absence of petticoats altogether must be carefully avoided". Complicated devices were resorted to in the attempt to hold the skirts in place in all circumstances with various forms of straps. Some experts recommended a leather strap holding all the skirts together and fastened round the lady's thighs, which must have been remarkably uncomfortable, or pinning the different layers to each other. A French Royal Master of the Horse, L.H. de Pons d'Hostor, pointed out in his book that such methods could be dangerous and instead advised his pupils:

"... lightly to sew a ribbon on the over-skirt and to pass this

"Mrs. Welby on a bay hunter in the grounds of Allington Hall" by John Ferneley Snr. 1853. (*Courtesy of Richard Green Galleries, London.*)

over the left foot like a stirrup. All the skirts will now be held in place by the outer one, and the wind, becoming more timid, will not be able to play with them more violently than it does with your veil."

Not only such fastenings were dangerous in the event of a fall. Almost anything in the voluminous, flowing mass could become entangled or caught up and cause a very nasty accident. The only redeeming feature was that everything was of such flimsy material that it was likely to tear if caught. Few contemporaries would have been consoled by this reflection, as most were more concerned with decency than safety.

Only after some time did a whip become an acceptable part of women's equipment. Whilst this is today seen as an even more important aid for the side saddle rider than for the cross saddle, being used on the offside to counteract the absence of a leg, the whips carried in the early 19th century appear more decorative than practical. Indeed in many of the pictures in which they are shown they are either dangling ineffectively or held out at a nonchalant angle. More serious-minded ladies would carry theirs rigidly erect in front of them in a military if equally impractical fashion.

So the development of hunting in its modern form found women singularly ill-equipped to take advantage of it. If such hardy spirits as Lady Lade and Lady Salisbury had been unusual in their determination to ride as well as any man before the revolution in the hunting field, the struggle became that much harder after the new emphasis on pace, and galloping on over fences. There was no improvement during the next thirty years, with more and more land being enclosed, creating an increasing number of fences to be jumped with all the handicaps to which women were subject.

Another problem for women coming hard on the heels of enclosures was that, as the newly-planted quickthorn hedges grew up they became "bullfinches", unjumpably tall and prickly, which a horse jumped through rather than over, ruining many a man's silk hat and threatening dreadful vengeance to a woman's face. In time though, the fences were cut and laid, becoming more solid and formidable obstacles, but less damaging to the complexion. Even where they remained bullfinches, older fences almost always have gaps and thin places in them, whereas a properly tended young hedge can present an almost impenetrable barrier.

Psychologically also a vicious circle was established, particularly in the more fashionable hunting countries, which spread outwards to the provinces. Visitors came, first to Melton Mowbray, and later also to Market Harborough, Rugby, Northampton, and Leamington, for the particular purpose of hunting. They would base themselves in these towns for the whole of the hunting season, so that the society in these places was almost exclusively male. This led to the feeling amongst both men and women that the hunting field was no more a fit place for a woman than the interior of a gentleman's club, or, until recently, the common room of one of the older Oxford or Cambridge colleges, or any of the other male bastions which have but lately fallen to, or are still resisting, female attack.

When Mr. Meynell was Master of the Quorn, those wishing to hunt with him from some distance away would come and stay either in his own house at Quorndon, where one of his servants was authorised to run a sort of private catering business for the needs of the visitors, or somewhere else close by. The brother of the famous north country Master of Hounds Ralph Lambton is generally credited with being the first to establish himself in Melton specifically for the hunting, probably around 1790. His reason, strange to later ears, was that he found life around Quorn too boisterous in the evenings and so chose "the unfrequented town of Melton". Others soon saw the advantages of Melton Mowbray, which was within reach of the Belvoir and what later became the Cottesmore Hounds as well as Mr. Meynell's, and soon the habit of taking a house or lodgings in that town for the hunting season became widespread.

This was a bachelor way of life: virtually no women considered coming or would have been welcomed at this time. One who did attempt it around 1812 was the courtesan Harriette Wilson, not through any wish to take part in the hunting, but in pursuit of her current lover. She soon found the Meltonians led what she "considered a very stupid life. They were off at six in the morning, dressed up in old single-breasted coats that had once been red, and came back to dinner at six", after which, by her account, some sneaked out after "a few wretched, squalid prostitutes". Harriette Wilson was out to see the worst of what happened: even so there is little doubt that much of Meltonian society would not have welcomed the presence of ladies. Too much alcohol was consumed, and the wilder element, sometimes, particularly if there was a frost, insufficiently occupied, certainly found some outlandish forms of entertainment.

The "Mad" Marquess of Waterford led a group of kindred spirits in a series of exploits which make the behaviour of many a modern football hooligan appear restrained and reasonable. Fortunately most Meltonians did not share their belief in a divine right going with their money and titles to subordinate other people's well-being to their own high spirits. One evening they literally painted the town red, going out with paint pots and brushes, quite prepared to beat up anyone who interfered. On another occasion Waterford won a bet at a dinner party at his house at Lowesby by having a gate fixed up in the middle of the dining room, bringing in a favourite horse and jumping the gate, which is still at Lowesby, measuring four feet in height. Another horse which was the unfortunate subject of a bet found itself taken upstairs to the first floor of a house. However it was quite determined not to go down again, and, some days later, was bought where it stood and eventually rescued with expensive equipment by the removal of a window, to be renamed First Flight. Altogether Melton society was not such as to welcome ladies.

Nor was it only in the Shires that a few wild spirits gave hunting men everywhere a generally quite undeserved reputation for wild living. The excesses of the wildest Meltonians pale before those of John Mytton of Halston in Shropshire, father of Mrs. Poulett Somerset. His idea of a practical joke was to put a guest, who had dined too well to make his way home, to bed with two bulldogs and a bear. Another time he gave a creditor calling for his money a note to take to a named person; the man was governor of a lunatic asylum, the note an instruction to "admit the bearer". One of his dinner parties was enlivened by his appearance in the dining room in full hunting dress, mounted on a bear. All went well till he applied the spurs, when the bear promptly bit him.

Such behaviour was the exception not the rule even in the Shires. Certainly throughout most of hunting England, where few if any visitors came expressly for the hunting, there was no reason to think that those men who hunted in any way behaved worse than their contemporaries who did not. Indeed, as Gaston de Foix had written more than four hundred years earlier, a strong case can be argued that "hunting causeth a man to eschew the seven deadly sins". All the same, talk of such episodes must have caused many a mother to welcome the restrictions of saddle and dress which prevented her daughters from following their brothers into the hunting field. There was a strong feeling at this time that only women of doubtful virtue would consider hunting.

"The Herefordshire Hounds at Hampton Court, Herefordshire. The lady is Mrs. Arkwright" by M.F. Morgan. (*Courtesy of Fores Gallery Ltd.*)

---

There was one exception to this. It was quite acceptable for the wives and daughters of Masters of Hounds to take an interest in the sport. If for the reasons already given almost all restricted such interest to a quiet ride to the meet and gentle hack home again, there were a few brave exceptions. Most conspicuous amongst these were the wife and daughters of the First Duke of Cleveland (or Marquess at the time when Nimrod visited him), whose Raby Hounds hunted an immense tract of country in the North of England, comprising most of what are now the Zetland, Bedale and Hurworth countries and part of the Badsworth.

"Nimrod," (Charles James Apperley, the famous hunting correspondent) had a few days with the Raby Hounds on one of his hunting tours in 1826 and was clearly much impressed by the performance of the female side of the family in the hunting field. The Marchioness of Cleveland at this time was not the Duke's first wife, the mother of his daughters. She was the former Elizabeth Russell, daughter of a market gardener, who earned herself a considerable notoriety living under the protection of a succession of well-known men before eventually marrying the future Duke of Cleveland in 1813. Cynics would say she was precisely the sort of woman one would expect to find in the hunting field at that time. The Duke clearly was, in regard to women in the hunting field if in no other respect, a remarkably enlightened man. At the time of Nimrod's visit two daughters, one married, one unmarried, as well as his wife, were hunting. There was also a Mrs. Wilkinson out, and apparently some eight horses were kept for the use of the ladies. The Marchioness would visit her favourite horse, Raby, who had never given her a fall, in the stables daily and feed him on plum bread.

The performance of the ladies in the field impressed Nimrod, even allowing for his bias in favour of his host's family and his snobbish predilection to a title.

> "Lady Augusta Milbanke rode a thoroughbred horse, formerly in Mr. Maxse's stable, and one which but few women would have nerve for. He likes to go quick at his fences, but her ladyship's hand was quite a match for him, and I saw him very well piloted over two or three awkward places."

So these girls at any rate, dressed in their scarlet habits, were evidently riding to hounds and not simply appearing at the meet. Perhaps on this occasion the Marchioness was not going so well: Nimrod describes her as a "most graceful horsewoman; and when her favourite hunter, Brighton, was in his prime, cut a prominent figure in 'The Operations of the Raby Pack'."

Nimrod cannot conceal his surprise at such feminine participation.

> "The Ladies Augusta Milbanke and Arabella Vane are constant attendants of the Raby Pack three times a fortnight, which is pretty good work for the softer sex. They have been well entered to hounds from their very infancy; yet" [this word betrays the attitude of the times] "it would be difficult to produce two more amiable or accomplished persons. As for Lady Augusta, she is

> not only a fine rider, but she is nothing less than a sportswoman. She is as attentive to hounds in their work as her noble father himself, and he never enjoyed a fine run more. Then look at the elegant and delicate Lady Arabella Vane, of whom it may be said, a hundred years hence . . ." [he quotes a Latin tag which indicates that she is not more conspicuous by her birth than her accomplishments] "and who will say that foxhunting abates a woman's softness?"

Evidently many did say so. Ladies of sufficient glamour and charm, and particularly foreign ones, can sometimes break all the rules. Mrs. Shakerley was not the wife or daughter of a Master of Hounds, and there are no grounds for casting doubts on her virtue, yet her appearance in the hunting field in 1825 earned nothing but enthusiasm from Nimrod. He wrote after a day with the Warwickshire: "There was to me, and indeed it must have been to everyone, a very agreeable sight on this day in the field. This was Mrs. Shakerley (the lady of Mr. Shakerley, jun., of Somerford Hall, Cheshire) upon her beautiful, I might almost say superb, horse, The Golden Ball. Mrs. Shakerley is a French lady of high birth, and certainly the most graceful horsewoman I ever saw upon a horse: the Lady Eveline herself, on her white palfrey, could not have excelled her. Her hand, as well as her seat, is quite perfect, and I understand she has gone very well once or twice in Leicestershire."

Mrs. Shakerley and the Duke of Cleveland's family were exceptional. Most of Nimrod's other references to ladies confirm the impression that their part in the day finished after the meet: "Met at Kettleby where at least three hundred horses were assembled with a pretty sprinkling of ladies"; "Ladies were often of the party, though they never quitted the carriages", much the most usual way for ladies to attend a meet.

Lack of ladies in the field in no way indicated a lack of female support for hunting. Nimrod, on visiting the Hurworth kennel, which was not administered on the grand lines of Leicestershire, Raby or other smart establishments, was amused by Tommy and his wife. Tommy (to Nimrod's surprise) combined the jobs of whipper-in and feeder, and lived with his wife and six children so close to the kennels that there was a trap door by the head of their bed which they could open and rate hounds through it

"Thomas Tertius Paget M.P. and his Wife" by Ferneley.
*(Photograph by courtesy of Sotheby's.)*

should the noise become excessive! Since Nimrod assures us that the smell was like lavender water to them, if he spoke to Tommy's wife at all, she must have given the impression of sharing her husband's enthusiasm for hounds. No doubt for every woman mystified and irritated by her menfolk's hunting there was another like Tommy's wife who may never have sat on a horse, but did more for hunting, behind the scenes, than all the smart young men overriding hounds in Leicestershire.

For the limitations on women riding to hounds did not prevent them from taking an interest in hound work and hunting. "Cecil" talks of a Mrs. Vickers and her niece Miss Miller in the Albrighton country in the early 1830s who "were most determined admirers of foxhunting and generally met the hounds whenever they were within reasonable distance". The image is of ladies keen to see hounds working, but not to ride across a country, using their horses as their modern equivalents might use a motor car. The form their interest took was a strange one: Mrs. Vickers had a tame vixen which was allowed to go off annually in search of a mate and Mrs. Vickers delighted to see the resulting litter of semi-wild cubs hunted when the time came. Apart from the dubious ethics of the proceeding, it was, hardly surprisingly, not productive of any outstanding sport.

Women in the hunting field who were not sufficiently outstanding to demand unmixed admiration provoked some amused mockery. In 1826 a Captain Russell, whose letters are quoted in C.D. Ellis' book *Leicestershire and the Quorn Hunt*, wrote to his wife after a day with the Belvoir: "We had a fine morning and Lady Elizabeth Belgrave was out galloping about, but the afternoon grew cold and stormy." He was equally disparaging when he had been out with the Cottesmore: "We had Lady Eleanor Lowther out today, in a scarlet riding habit, looking like the rising sun." This Lady Eleanor was originally Lady Lucy Eleanor Sherard, daughter of the Earl of Harborough, and in 1817 had married Colonel Henry Lowther, whose father was Master of the Cottesmore. At the same period both her mother-in-law Lady Lonsdale and sister-in-law Lady Frederick Bentinck came out with hounds in red habits, as befitted the ladies of the Master's family at the time.

There seems little doubt that the story told by the immortal rough rider, Dick Christian, also relates to this Lady Eleanor, although it is often referred to her daughter and namesake, who later married John Talbot Clifton. However the daughter would not have been *Lady* Eleanor Lowther, and Christian's opening words refer to "poor Lady Eleanor Lowther", more likely a reference to one dead when he told the story, as the mother would have been, and the daughter would not. Dick Christian, who lived from 1779 to 1862, right through the Golden Age of hunting in the Shires, was perhaps the finest rider across Leicestershire of them all, for, as a professional, his horses were never the polished performers enjoyed by other Meltonians. In his old age, he was sought out by the writer Henry Hall Dixon, known as the Druid, and his reminiscences published. In these he tells the story of Lady Eleanor:

> "That minds me of poor Lady Eleanor Lowther. What a thing I once see her do! She come to the very steepest part of Bur-

rough Hill, close to the hounds, and she says to me, 'Richard! If you will go up here with the hounds, I'll follow you.' Near the top, hang me, if I didn't think she and the horse would be over backwards. I says, 'Do, my lady, catch hold of your horse's mane, and lean forwards more.' So we gets up safe, and they all went round, and my word, the gentlemen did stare when they see us."

"By Your Leave" by F.C. Turner. 1845.
(*Courtesy of Arthur Ackermann & Son Ltd.*)

Christian was clearly an admirer of women in the hunting field. He says of a Miss Milbanke: "What a clipping rider she was with the Rufford! Such a seat and hands; I never see her beat by none of them." Lady Eleanor, for whose husband's family Christian had worked, early in his career, as whipper-in, was not the only lady he had to pilot. Perhaps around 1820, after the death of Christian's first wife, whom he had married before he was twenty years old and who bore him twenty children before her death, Dick was asked to pilot a certain Miss Redfern, whose father had a house near Melton. Mr. Redfern was undeterred by tales of the undesirability of hunting for young ladies, but in his case the worst predictions of friends and neighbours proved justified. The girl fell in love with her pilot, and Christian found the idea of marriage as attractive as she did. Her father's fury was not sufficient to deter such a dashing couple: Dick, in the most traditional romantic style, put a ladder up to her window and waited below with the horse. Sadly, she lived long enough to bear him but a single daughter: for his third wife Christian selected a Belgian tightrope dancer.

The story is told of a certain young lady some time well before 1835, who had hunted all her life with the West country pack where she had been brought up. Possibly the girl's father held the Mastership of the hounds, which are unnamed. Certainly she had, as Nimrod would say, been well entered to hounds from her very infancy. She was staying in Bath, where she had been hailed as a belle, but, perhaps feeling that a season with the Beaufort would be more fun than a season in Bath, set out for her first day with them. As hounds were drawing she gave a ringing holloa. The Duke came over with a mystified expression: it was quite bad enough having women out without them interfering in the proceedings.

"How did you know it was a fox?" he demanded.

"Because I rode in upon his back and unkennelled him, and he has gone down wind to Badminton," replied the girl.

Quite won over by such an impressively technical explanation, the Duke indicated his satisfaction to his huntsman who brought hounds over, they streamed away on the line she had pointed out, and an outstanding hunt followed, "through the whole of which the unremitting attention of the Duke to the fair Amazon, whose side he never quitted, added not a little to her enjoyment; nor was she at all at a loss, or behindhand, in urging her steed over wall or fence, the Duke being her leader."

The same girl, perhaps on her return home from Bath, had won the heart of an extremely smart young man about town. When he came to stay with her parents she resolved that only the best was good enough for her admirer. The North Devon Staghounds were meeting near by next morning, so she generously mounted him on her favourite mare, taking another horse for herself. Before ever they reached hounds, they crossed a field which had been divided up by the farmer with temporary fencing for his sheep. She popped over the fence but, turning, saw to her amazement that the terrified young man had not allowed the mare to approach it.

> "Thus destined either to lose the day's sport, or proceed alone, (she) at once adopted the latter alternative, and, cantering gaily on, turned to wave her adieus to her London lover, whose last fond glance – in her own words – was directed to her from the *wrong* side of the sheep hurdles."

When she returned home that night she found that the young man, unable to bear the mockery of the rest of the party, had set out for London immediately.

So for the small number of women and girls who got everything right, looks, turnout, the way they rode and above all behaviour on and off the hunting field, hunting was acceptable. In practice, virtually all those who achieved this were close connections of Masters, preferably daughters rather than wives, enabling them to learn the right way to do everything from childhood. There was still too high a proportion of those appearing in the hunting field at all who did so often for the wrong reasons, or whose reputations off the hunting field were too bad to be redeemed by the way they went on it. So hunting continued to be frowned on for many a girl keen to try.

Nellie Holmes, for instance, was described in 1841 as "topping the fences like a bird, to the admiration of all", and was, according to "Gumley" Wilson in his book *Green Peas at Christmas*, the only woman riding in the Shires at that time (1832–43). "She was the best horsewoman I ever saw before or since – hand, seat, judgment and resolution perfect", but unfortunately her private life was too well known for her example to be one young girls would be urged to follow. Starting life as Eleanor Sutor, she swiftly made her reputation as a woman of the town, eventually becoming Lady Rivers. *The Sporting Magazine* reported that: "though we have seen some ladies go uncommonly well across country, we frankly confess she transcends them all, and shines the Dian of the Chase. Alas that she is no Diana!"

Others came out with their interest limited even on the day to the pursuit of men rather than of the fox. Although the pianist Clari:

> ". . . rode intrepidly . . . well mounted, with an ostrich feather in her beaver, she flew like Camilla, with a host of flatterers in her train. On the fox breaking cover, those old in the sport shot away like lightning, leaving the captivated beaux entangled

in the toils of love, so great is the charm of beauty's power."

One lady who succeeded in winning universal acclaim over a remarkably long period was Mrs. Turner Farley. She enjoyed the distinction of being the only lady to whom Thomas Assheton Smith, acknowledged by his contemporaries as being the greatest rider to hounds of them all, gave his much sought after hunt button. She and her husband had followed Assheton Smith round the country in his different Masterships: the Quorn 1806–16 (or 17), the Burton 1816–24 and the Tedworth Hounds 1826–58. She was still alive, though no longer riding, in 1879 when Lady Augusta Fane first arrived in Leicestershire as a young girl and was taken with her sister to dine at Wartnaby Hall (a haunted house, so the old lady's granddaughter told Lady Augusta) where Mrs. Turner Farley then lived with her son.

Lady Augusta, living in the age of side saddles with a leaping head and habits similar to those worn by women side saddle today, was particularly intrigued to be shown all the old equipment. "The saddles were a wonderful sight, the seats scooped out, very high in front, with only two narrow pommels on each side and a stirrup firmly strapped round with the girths. Her habits were made of fine face-cloth, and a long full flowing skirt. Her jacket had lapels, and with this she wore an embroidered collar fastened by a cameo brooch. She had tight riding breeches and over them a white petticoat with a lace flounce, and her hat had a long feather hanging at the side. I suppose women did not realise the danger of riding in these voluminous skirts, as Mrs. Farley, the Dowager Lady Yarborough, and many others who wore them, rode fearlessly to hounds."

Mrs. Farley had breeches whilst retaining the frilly white petticoat: some women abandoned the petticoat in favour of white linen pantaloons before they started to wear sensible breeches at all. Perhaps hers was a reasonable compromise for the day between what was essential for an elegant lady and what was practical for one keen to ride to hounds. Mrs. Farley clearly made a tremendous impression on Lady Augusta.

> "She had masses of silver hair which came down to her knees. She impressed on her friends that she owed her splendid health to the fact that every night she took a dose of two grains of

"Portrait of Lady Broughton" by A.F. de Prades. 1861. (*Courtesy of Arthur Ackermann & Son Ltd.*)

calomel, but I think she must have possessed a marvellous constitution to stand such drastic treatment."

Even the most old fashioned of hunting men were prepared to make exceptions in favour of individual women who won them over. Charles Davis, the unbending straight-laced professional huntsman of the Royal Buckhounds, which hunted carted deer close to London, exempted a certain Miss Gilbert from his general disapproval of women hunting "on account of her cheerful spirit and dashing riding . . . but especially on account of her Spartan endurance of long rides home at hounds' pace, of which he himself was a great exponent", according to a later Master, Lord Ribblesdale. But even then, the country, Lord Ribblesdale tells us, "only presented average opportunities either for falls or for conspicuous exploits."

There is no doubt that the odds in the first half of the 19th century were heavily stacked against the girl contemplating riding to hounds. Should she overcome almost inevitable strong parental disapproval and male opposition ("I may state, as a well known fact, that the opinions of the opposite sex are generally adverse to their partaking of the sport", wrote Mrs. Russell Clarke in her book *The Habit and the Horse* in 1860) the girl had still to contend with the hazards of quite unsuitable clothes and a saddle on which it was almost impossible to jump a fence without a hand to hold on by. Whilst the disapproving majority were quick to point out the dangers inherent in the sport, there seems to have been little conception of the connection between these material and alterable conditions and the creation of risk.

The point certainly escaped "Gumley" Wilson. By the time he wrote his book in 1882 most of these artificial hazards had been done away with, yet he continued to feel as he had done in the '30s (except when dazzled by the charms of Nellie Holmes):

> "In those days few if any women hunted, and the Shires are certainly not in my opinion adapted to female equestrianism, to coin a word. A woman may ride over a country with some safety, but riding through it is quite another matter. Bullfinches which close up after you pass through are ugly customers for a woman on a side saddle – specially with a ditch on the far side, and I have seen more than once a woman pulled off her saddle and deposited in the ditch and in some cases with the horse on her. The fact is I hate to see a woman ride to hounds in the Shires; I know the danger which few women realise. . . . Since those days hunting fields have been full of riding women, and some have come to grief, the result of which they will no doubt feel for years."

The female point of view was clearly expressed around 1860 by a more thoughtful man, Whyte-Melville, though he puts the words into the mouth of his heroine, Kate Coventry:

> "They get us a side saddle, as they call it, of enormous weight and inconvenience, on which they plant pommels enough to impale three women; they place us in an attitude from which it is next to impossible to control a horse should he be violent, and in a dress which ensures a horrible accident should he fall, added to which, they constantly give us the worst quadruped in the stable; and yet, with all these drawbacks, such is our own innate talent and capacity, we ride many an impetuous steed in safety and comfort that a man would find a dangerous and incontrollable 'mount'. For my part, I only wish I had been born a man. . . ."

All these disadvantages provided the reasons why women should not hunt, and undoubtedly kept a small number of women out of the hunting field. The reason the vast majority of women in fact did not hunt was more general: in Victorian times and before there were many things, including most forms of sporting activity, which women simply did not do. Many of these sporting taboos have only been broken down in our own generation. Women have only just begun to ride in races other than point-to-points. Even today the number of women who shoot compared with men is remarkably small. In the 19th century few forms of sport were generally considered desirable for a girl to participate in, with the exception of croquet, and up to the middle of the century and beyond hunting was certainly not one of them.

A few brave souls made the grade in the face of all these hazards. Most of those who did had the unusual benefit of some form of family support, from parents or husband, and even for them it must have been a tremendous struggle. Mrs. Russell Clarke, after summing up much of the disapproval, admits that she herself did a great deal of hunting in her youth, but advocates, wisely in the prevailing conditions, that only the best of horsewomen should make the attempt. A later writer complains that to keep beginners from the hunting field is like ruling that the water is too dangerous to enter before the child can swim. But undoubtedly up to about 1860 the hunting field was a dangerous place for the inexperienced woman, and no more to be recommended than a novice today should be advised to ride around Badminton or enter a point-to-point.

Yet a mere two decades later the whole position had changed. Just as at the beginning of the century improvements in hound breeding, enclosures and William Childe's discovery of a new way to ride across country had combined to revolutionise hunting for men, so now the invention of the leaping head, the modification of the habit and the example of an Empress did the same for women.

CHAPTER FOUR

# *THE COURTESAN AND THE EMPRESS*

Jules Charles Pellier is not a well known name. Yet his invention, made in collaboration with François Baucher, revolutionised the whole relationship between women and the horse. This remarkable innovation was the leaping head, or third pommel.

Side saddles before this time had two pommels, one on either side of the right leg. The third pommel was added below the other two, enabling it to come into contact with the left, not the right, leg. The pommel above the right leg was subsequently found to be unnecessary and abandoned, so that modern side saddles once again have two pommels, the lower of the two being the revolutionary and all-important leaping head.

This device, when correctly fitted, does not come into contact with the leg except when jumping or in emergency. However, it is close enough for contact to be achieved effortlessly on those occasions and enables the rider to have a strong, independent seat. Although invented as early as 1830 in France, it took some considerable time to come into universal use. Criticism that it could cause the rider to be hung up was eventually rejected, this pommel creating no greater danger than the original two. Indeed this risk was reduced when the upper, right-hand pommel was discontinued. Women were, however, frequently advised in the early days to learn to ride first without this new aid, to render them independent of it should some inexplicable accident deprive them of its assistance.

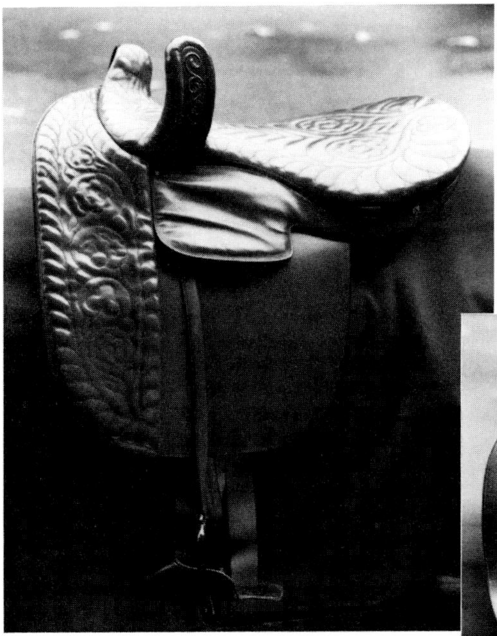

*Top* "Queen Victoria's side saddle with pommels in the old-fashioned position without a leaping head, and with a slipper stirrup. The rose, thistle and shamrock are worked into the leather." (*Photograph by Sir Anthony Rawlinson.*)
*Bottom* "Side saddle of Her Majesty the Queen and used by her for the Trooping of the Colour. This is a side saddle of the modern type, the lower pommel being the leaping head." (*Photograph by Sir Anthony Rawlinson.*)

The effect its adoption could have is well illustrated in Mary Richardson's book, *The Life of a Great Sportsman*, her biography of her brother, John Maunsell Richardson, who twice rode the winner of the Grand National. Richardson eventually married the widowed Victoria, Countess of Yarborough, and the writer tells of her early meetings with her future sister-in-law, then Lady Worsley, when she herself was but eleven years old and Lady Worsley eighteen. When the future Countess (her father-in-law, the Earl of Yarborough, was still alive at the time) first arrived in the Brocklesby country with her husband for the 1859–60 season they caused a tremendous stir. Old Lord Yarborough, whilst retaining the Mastership nominally, appeared but infrequently, and the Brocklesby Hounds were in the charge of the professional huntsman. When the young bride not only showed her enthusiasm for life in the country and hunting in particular, but proved that she intended to ride to hounds as well as the men, local enthusiasm was unbounded. The eleven-year-old Mary Richardson, brought up with her brothers to enjoy hounds and horses as they did, soon hero worshipped her absolutely.

Mary had recently been given a new saddle as a birthday present. Delighted though she was with it, she did not at first appreciate how special it was. It had three pommels. When her heroine one day remarked on Mary's remarkable ability to jump fences without a hand on the back of the saddle, a thing the older girl had never achieved, she at first, child-like, attributed it to her own superior horsemanship. Then she thought of her new saddle and described it. Victoria was fascinated: apparently she had never seen or heard of any such thing. Finally the child jumped off her pony to show the saddle, and soon found herself promising to lend it to her heroine for a day's hunting. Not surprisingly, an order immediately went out from Brocklesby, and the days of jumping fences with a supporting hand were over.

It is interesting that such an eminent proponent of the art of riding across a country should, as late as 1860, previously have been unaware of the existence of saddles with three pommels, and particularly creditable that she had already made her name before acquiring one. But Victoria, Countess of Yarborough was a remarkable woman. She subsequently took on the Mastership of the Brocklesby Hounds from 1875 to 1880, after the deaths of her father-in-law and husband, during her son's minority, even carrying the horn with the dog pack at one stage. Later still, she and her second husband moved to Leicestershire, where she followed him over everything, including the "dread Whissendine" on two occasions. She is also said by her efficient management to have paid off mortgages of £100,000 on the Brocklesby estate during her son's minority and was equally successful as Honorary Colonel of the First Lincolnshire Light Horse, appearing in camp, according to the newspapers, "dressed in the tunic, cross belt and sword and wearing the colours of the troop . . . (and) . . . occupied a leading place in the march". Such exotic dress clearly appealed to her, and she is equally decoratively, if impractically, turned out for hunting in the painting of her by Sir Francis Grant presented by the Brocklesby tenants.

Lady Yarborough was of the generation which viewed the introduction of a so-called "safety skirt" with scorn, dubbing it "the fig leaf". Whilst Lady Augusta Fane reports that this was first introduced around 1875, when Mrs. Arthur was one of the first to adopt it in the Shires, it was in fact in use at least fifteen years earlier. There is a Leech cartoon in *Punch* in 1860: "Miss Diana strips off at a fence and leaves the better half of her habit on the pommels of her saddle." For the principle of the safety skirt was that it came off in case of emergency. This earned it the disapproval of all those more concerned with decorum than safety, and later generations regarded it as clumsy and unattractive, which indeed it was in comparison with the superbly tailored skirts which succeeded it. There was a slit at the back which was opened on mounting and fastened again immediately the rider returned to the ground. The careful fitting of the skirt to the shape of the knee was a refinement unknown at this stage, however, and indeed difficult to introduce whilst there were still three pommels on the saddle. The safety skirt, if expertly cut, made of sufficiently heavy material, and held down with elastic, looked reasonable whilst the woman was in the saddle, so long as she did not allow her foot to poke forward. When on foot, it contained too much material ever to look other than strange, for this quantity of fabric was necessary to ensure that there should never be the briefest exposure of the woman's legs when dismounting. At the turn of the century such false modesty was put aside.

Thus the garment in which Mrs. Arthur caused such a sensation around 1875 was one which a mere quarter of a century later would seem old fashioned and over modest. But Mrs. Arthur's early appearances in the "fig leaf" safety skirt caused her to be "cut" by other women for indecent behaviour. Fortunately she was a woman of considerable strength of mind, with the good sense to rate safety before a spurious respectability. She was described by a contemporary as having an eye like a hawk and nerve like a lion, and was always ready to lend the huntsman a hand, being amongst the few women of the time to understand hunting as well as riding.

Another improvement in the side saddle was the introduction of the balance strap. Balance straps were occasionally used early in the 19th century, but they did not come into general use until the middle of that century. This was a most important development, particularly from the horse's point of view. The strap, coming from the back of the saddle on the offside down to the line of the girth, and steadying the saddle, made sore backs, if unfortunately not obsolete, no longer an unavoidable hazard. Before this innovation, the only way grooms knew to avoid constant movement was to tighten the girths so excessively that horses would lie down or roll in an effort to escape the discomfort. Another benefit of the balance strap was that it enabled women to rise at the trot, a custom once frowned on for men as well as women, and one which was likely to result in disaster on a side saddle without a balance strap, almost certainly giving the horse a sore back and perhaps even causing the saddle to slip right round.

Around the same time as the leaping head was introduced, another impractical anachronism was at last done away with: the slipper stirrup. It was not yet replaced with a plain iron stirrup like that used by men: one heavily lined with leather or sheepskin was at first introduced. It was soon joined by a variety of patent safety stirrups of varying designs.

During the 1850s, the number of women hunting showed a marked increase. In *Mr. Sponge's Sporting Tour*, first published in 1853, Surtees takes it for granted that there may be a few ladies out with hounds, particularly in the more fashionable countries, though he also assumes that, with the notable exception of Lucy Glitters, they will not go well across country. It has been suggested that Lucy Glitters was modelled on Lady Lade. This is certainly more plausible than the more popular theory identifying her with Skittles, who, as we shall see, did not appear in the hunting field

"Lucy Glitters Showing the Way" by John Leech from *Mr. Sponge's Sporting Tour* by R.S. Surtees.

until after the appearance of her fictional counterpart in print. Surtees summed up his attitude thus:

"When women do ride they generally ride like the very devil. There is no medium with them. They either 'go' to beat the men or they don't 'go' at all."

Whyte-Melville's outlook is similar, once more conceding that there were occasional women, such as Kate Coventry, who did compete with the men. His less dashing heroine Cissy Dove in *Market Harborough* was based on Constance Humfrey, niece of the Reverend Cave Humfrey, incumbent of Laughton and Foxton near Market Harborough, and model for Parson Dove. Constance Humfrey habitually hunted with her uncle dressed in a fawn-coloured habit, from which Whyte-Melville derived the name of Dove.

A book published in 1860 states that: "In almost every part of the country two or three ladies are to be found who greatly distinguish themselves in the hunting field, and who are regarded with just pride by the hunts to which they belong." Anthony Trollope, in his *Hunting Sketches* first published in 1865, takes it for granted that women will hunt, and that "the number of such ladies is very much on the increase." By and large, he welcomes this tendency, believing that it takes "off from hunting that character of horseyness", though he has reservations about the sort of woman who constantly demands assistance. He also makes the point that any woman who hunts must really enjoy it, as there is so much pressure against her hunting, and no extraneous reasons for women, unlike men, to appear in the hunting field. Surtees does not accept this, believing that many of them hunt because there is a rich, young bachelor Master, or for some similar reason.

GONE AWAY!

*Old Coachman.* "Now, Miss Ellen! Miss Ellen! You know what your Pa said! You was to take the greatest Care of Jory!"——
*Miss Ellen.* "So I will, Robert! and that's why I am Taking him off the nasty Hard Road, Poor Thing!"

"Gone Away!" by John Leech.

Lady Augusta Fane writes that she does not believe any ladies hunted regularly from Melton before 1850. One of the first to do so was Lady Grey de Wilton, who reigned as uncrowned Queen of Melton for some sixty years. John Maunsell Richardson said that she, in common with his own wife Victoria, Lady Yarborough (she retained the title even after her second marriage) and Lady Alexander Paget, was quite capable of holding her own with any of the men. She sat absolutely straight, had a superb figure, was beautifully turned out and looked magnificent on a horse. She is also credited with a remarkable memory for a horse, recognising it years later even if she had only seen it once. A charming and amusing hostess, she remained at Melton for the rest of her life, marrying Arthur Pryor after the death of her first husband, and still at least attending the meet mounted at the age of eighty. She lived until 1919. Her father-in-law, the "Wicked" Earl of Wilton, was known as King of Melton, a strange man of extraordinary influence, a superb rider to hounds, whose life Lady Augusta described as being a "curious mixture of religion, sport and vice". Lord Wilton, however, believed in the maintenance of old-fashioned standards for women in the hunting field. One day he came home from hunting shattered after seeing two ladies: "I am sure you will not believe it, but I saw the ankle of one of those two young ladies, and besides that I heard one of them call her horse a devil, and distinctly heard the other say 'damn'!" The unfortunate girls were known as Devil and Damn for many years afterwards.

"An Incident in a Hunt with the Quorn in the Merry Sixties" from *Chit Chat* by Lady Augusta Fane.

In one way the hunting field was becoming an increasingly respectable place for a woman to appear. Even Queen Victoria was seen out with the Belvoir Hounds in the 1850s, though she may only have been to the meet. But the growing numbers inevitably led to much talk of romance in the hunting field. There were many jokes about halters and altars, bridles and bridals and Fast Things across a country.

One of the more dramatic elopements to follow a hunting field romance concerned the "beautiful daughter of a 'proud and mighty' Scottish noble" and a handsome but penniless young English subaltern named Bob, who was stationed near the girl's home. On the girl's father refusing to allow her to consider the young man's proposal, they decided to elope, galloping away from the hunting field to be married in their hunting clothes.

Meanwhile, when the girl failed to return home, her suspicious father made enquiries and set off in pursuit, catching up with them at an inn where they were resting, and hammered on the door demanding to be let in. The girl knew more of Scottish marriage law than her bridegroom, and realised that the marriage was not valid until it was consummated. She drew the curtains and leaped into bed, calling, "Quick Bob, into bed, boots and all Bob!" Not only was their marriage a resounding success, but her father soon became reconciled and was later as pleased as anyone that he had been just too late.

J.M.K. Elliott wrote of his experience with the Grafton in the middle of the 19th century. He later piloted many women, including the Queen of Naples and, briefly, her sister the Empress Elizabeth of Austria, and makes the point that a pilot is necessary not because he can ride better, but because he can do things the lady cannot manage. Getting off to open a heavy gate, for example, is no job for anyone on a side saddle. Amongst the ladies he most admired earlier in his career was Mrs. Jack Villiers, an outstanding horsewoman, who was left a widow at an early age with immense debts incurred by her late husband. She did not appear again until she was in a position to pay all that was owed. On her next visit to Melton after that they rang the church bells in appreciation, and when she needed a pilot the famous Jem Mason, winner of the first Grand National on Lottery, volunteered.

Jem Mason piloted two different ladies on alternate days with Mr. Tailby's Hounds (now the Fernie). One day it would be Mrs.

Villiers and on the other he was followed by an equally outstanding horsewoman, if less reputable character, the redoubtable Skittles. Skittles' real name was Catherine Walters. She was born in Liverpool dockland in 1839. In the squalid atmosphere of her childhood, beauty was rare, and charm, vivacity and sparkle almost unknown. Catherine had all these qualities in abundance. One of her earliest and more innocent ways of making money earned her the nickname she kept for a lifetime. Many of the public houses provided an additional attraction in the form of a skittle alley, and in one such the child Catherine found employment. In the words of the popular song later written of her:

In Liverpool, in days gone by,
For ha'pence and her wittles,
A little girl by no means shy
Was settin' up the skittles.

She was only twelve when the family moved to Cheshire, where she first learned to ride. Perhaps she paid in the only way she knew. If this was what happened, she must have liked whoever helped her, for, professional though circumstances forced her to become, throughout her life she had too much pride and too much commonsense to sell herself to a man she disliked.

Soon her looks and personality, coupled with a natural chic and elegance which was later conspicuous even in the highest Parisian society, won her a lover of sufficient means to enable her to move to London. Here she found a new opening for her talents, including her horsemanship. London horse dealers in 1860 found the best way to sell a smart park hack or pair of carriage horses was to have them shown off in Rotten Row by those of the demi-monde who were sufficiently good horsewomen to sell their mounts as well as themselves. They were known as the pretty horsebreakers and Skittles was soon pre-eminent amongst them. The dealer with whom she was in partnership had her habits made by a leading tailor, and found he had little difficulty in selling a queer-tempered, hard mouthed brute as the perfect hack when shown off by Skittles. Soon she was driving a miniature phaeton drawn by tiny, high stepping chestnut ponies for which she was rumoured to be indebted, not to her dealer, but to a Russian prince.

Skittles first started hunting in the season of 1860–61. Her appearance in the hunting field led to what the Master described as a riot. She was hunting with Mr. Tailby's hounds in Leicestershire. So strongly was the presence of Catherine in the field resented that one nobleman threatened to warn hounds off his land if Mr. Tailby did not take hounds home whenever she came out. In his own words, Mr. Tailby took his stand on the broad principles that "the hunting field is open to all, that I am not the censor of the morality of the hunting field, that I have no right to disappoint others to gratify the prejudices of an individual, and that, in short, nothing could induce me to take hounds home merely because 'Skittles' is out. I am encouraged to this the more that I never hear any complaints of her conduct in the hunting field, or that she is in any way objectionable to the ladies who come out. On this I take my stand, let the result be what it may."

Indeed Skittles took great care not to cause offence or embarrassment. For example, she never stayed at a private house, but was often based at the Haycock Hotel at Wansford. Sir Arthur Hazlerigg was amongst those who defended her, saying that men took their wives to the theatre to see worse, and she would always be welcome at his home at Noseley in Mr. Tailby's country. One day when hounds were meeting at Noseley, her companion said to Skittles,

"Come on in: this is your best friend who says you are welcome."

"No," she replied, "I'll stop at the gate."

"Why?"

"Because he has a wife and daughters, and is the only real gentleman in Leicestershire."

On the other hand, Skittles was not prepared to be bullied by anyone. Lady Stamford, wife of the Master of the Quorn, was of similar background to Skittles herself. It was rumoured that she was the daughter of a Norfolk gamekeeper, or even of a gypsy, and that she had once worked in a circus, but jealousy of the superb way Skittles rode across a country spurred her to a high moral tone. When Skittles came to a meet of the Quorn, Lady Stamford entreated her husband to "dispatch that improper woman home". Skittles, considerate as ever, immediately turned to leave without more ado. But when on the way the fox crossed the road just in front of her with hounds in full cry, she could bear it no longer, jumped the fence off the road behind them and stayed with hounds for the rest of the hunt. Lord Stamford, quite won over, could only congratulate her, muttering "and damn all jealous women". Skittles merely laughed. "I don't know why she should give herself such airs: she's not even head of our profession: Lady Cardigan is."

The tall, slim, immaculately turned out Jem Mason made an appropriate companion for the beautiful Skittles. Both the glamour of their appearance and the coarseness of their conversation made a deep impression on one small boy. Years later he recalled watching the couple larking home after hunting:

"The man had a perfect seat, very upright, tall, thin and as smart as paint. His companion wore a habit that fitted her like a glove, and a bit of cherry ribbon round her neck. In short, she was a perfect dream. . . . She called out to her pilot . . . that when she reached home a certain portion of her anatomy would probably be of much the same hue as the tie she wore round her neck."

She was a remarkably dashing rider, once winning a hundred pounds in a bet by jumping some exceptionally high railings in Hyde Park. In her first hunting season she was amongst the spectators at the National Hunt Steeplechase at Farndon Field near Market Harborough. The brook in the course was such an awkward place that some of the riders objected to it, and a number of them had fallen there. After the race was over, Skittles created tremendous excitement by jumping it in cold blood.

After a traumatic affair with Lord Hartington, and a period of travel abroad, Skittles resolved to visit Paris. Soon her slim figure in its perfectly fitted habit and her superb horsemanship had captured as many hearts in the Bois de Boulogne as they had already done in Rotten Row. A contemporary recorded that "Skittles' pony chaise, with its pair of black cobs, and its two grooms on coal black cattle behind, beats everything from the Imperial stables". It was a remarkable achievement for a girl from the slums of Liverpool to have a distinguished French aristocrat pay tribute to her in these terms: "Quel chic! Quelle élégance! Quelle grâce à cheval!"

Catherine returned to Paris for another two or three summers, but was always back in Leicestershire in time for the hunting. Hearing one year that her old rival Lady Stamford had had a special habit made in dazzling blue velvet in which she planned to appear at the Opening Meet, Skittles paid a secret visit to her own tailor. When hounds met at Kirby Gate, Lady Stamford was not the

Skittles in the Bois de Boulogne.

centre of attention. Skittles was resplendent, appropriately, in a scarlet velvet habit. Lady Stamford, in a rage, sent her home, but

Lady Grey, who lived near by, invited her into her house to change into a less conspicuous outfit. Quickly rejoining the field, her triumph was complete at the end of the day when Lady Stamford unsuspectingly asked the identity of the young lady who had ridden so brilliantly in front of her throughout the hunt.

Some of her innovations in dress were more successful: she is credited with being the first to wear a silk hat and veil side saddle. Some amusement was had when Catherine had a fall and her skirt (presumably a "fig leaf") remained on the pommels of the saddle, leaving her in her petticoats. The cry went up for a married man to help her, and one confirmed old bachelor parson was much teased when he vehemently denied that he came in that category.

Amongst her numerous admirers in the Shires were the two Jewish brothers Behrens, who kept her park hack for her in the winter in such secrecy that the horse was only exercised at night. It was probably one of these two whom she was following when he fell into a brook in front of her. Jumping both brook and man, Skittles turned, kissed her hand and called, "Moses in the bulrushes, I see!"

Skittles lived until 1920, when she was eighty-one, deaf, partially blind and crippled by arthritis, but still enjoying the devotion and friendship of many of her old admirers. Her charm, good looks, quick wits, courage and kind heart mean that she is remembered more often and with more affection than any other woman who hunted in the last century, with only one exception.

That exception is the Empress Elizabeth of Austria. Hunting gave her perhaps the most complete happiness she knew in a tragic and bitter life. In turn, her beauty, charm and the way she rode to hounds combined to make Elizabeth a legend both in the Shires and later in Ireland.

Elizabeth of Wittelsbach was born in Bavaria in 1837. Her childhood was as free, wild and romantic as her nature craved, making the restraints which were later to be imposed on her by her role as Empress all the harder to bear. The castle at Possenhofen, with animals everywhere and a delightfully chaotic atmosphere, remained home to the Empress for the rest of her life. Frequently playing truant from the schoolroom, she played with her animals, explored the countryside and wrote romantic poetry. The only part of her education which was seriously attended to was her horsemanship. Her father, Duke Max, believed that his daughters as well as his sons should be taught to ride as beautifully as did he himself and Elizabeth was his star pupil. He remarked to her once: "If you and I, Sisi, had not been born princes, we would have been performers in a circus." All the girls' side saddles were made so that the pommels could be fixed on either side, giving them strong independent seats.

Elizabeth's first cousin was Franz Joseph, Emperor of Austria. Tall, good looking, hard working and devoted to his duty as he saw it, he was also an unreliable judge of character, rigid in outlook and prepared to sacrifice anything to "the glory of his dynasty and the greatness of his reign". Elizabeth was fifteen when she joined his party in the Austrian mountains. Her looks had developed to a stunning loveliness. She moved across the room as her father had taught her, not "strutting like princes or dragging her feet like common mortals, but like an angel with wings upon her feet". Despite her shyness, her mischievous vivacity won Franz Joseph's heart. When he who admired nothing in a woman so much as an elegant seat on a horse saw her ride, the conquest was complete. For all the tragedies and vicissitudes of their future life, he never ceased to love her. The fairytale romance was welcomed by everyone except the Emperor's hard-headed, far-seeing mother. Elizabeth also had her reservations: "If only he were not an Emperor," she whispered.

After her marriage, her selfish, freedom loving nature found the restrictions of her position intolerable. She was in continual conflict with her mother-in-law, allowed little part in the upbringing of her children and devastated by the death of her eldest daughter from measles. Her only pleasure seemed to be in taking longer and longer solitary rides. Soon she fled further from the stultifying atmosphere of the court, using her health as an excuse for extended visits far from Austria. She particularly enjoyed time spent in that problematical part of her husband's dominions, Hungary, where she was as deeply loved as she was resented in Austria. The Hungarians made her a present of a castle at Gödollo. Hunting was already a popular sport in Hungary, although there was little to jump. Elizabeth, who had first encountered the sport in Italy, introduced it at Gödollo, to the delight of the young Hungarians of her entourage. Here also she spent long hours in the riding school practising haute école and delighted in watching and entertaining professional circus riders. Her own horsemanship was remarkably advanced, including her approach to jumping. She noted in a book, "One must throw the body forward at the take-off", which was not a thing done by any of her English contemporaries.

Elizabeth's sister, the Queen of Naples, was the first to discover English hunting. She went well, provided she was mounted on the perfect horse, wrote her pilot. J.M.K. Elliott. Elizabeth, fired with enthusiasm by her sister's account and by a morning's cubhunting with the Belvoir during a visit to Britain, resolved to have a season in that country.

In March 1876 Elizabeth set off for England, where she rented Easton Neston, near Towcester, to hunt with the Grafton. On her first day she created a strong impression with the way she went over a big country in a fast hunt, and shortly afterwards the Grafton huntsman recorded that he, the Empress and her pilot were alone with hounds when her horse blew up. Next day she was invited to lunch at Althorp by Lord Spencer, the Master of the Pytchley, whom she had first met and entranced on her morning's cubhunting with the Belvoir. Spencer, a huge, red bearded leading Liberal politician, had recently returned to England after being a Viceroy of Ireland. His A.D.C. there had been a young officer known as "Bay" Middleton, who had moved to the Shires when Spencer left Ireland. Of all the brave wild young men crossing Ireland and the Shires, Bay rode the straightest and went the best. He was also a great steeplechase rider and cricketer. He derived almost equal amusement from "bear fights" with his friends, in which he was an implacable opponent, and such practical jokes as ripping a tail coat in two from behind. Yet on the whole he remained remarkably popular, perhaps because his laughter was not silenced when on one such occasion he found that his victim, forewarned, had taken the precaution of wearing a coat of Middleton's that evening. Wild, dashing, immaculately turned out and kindhearted if thoughtless, Bay's name had been linked with that of many a woman, some married. On his return from Ireland he became engaged to Charlotte Baird.

Ladies to Middleton were something entirely apart from the other excitements of life, the race course and the hunting field, where it was essential to be free in order to lead "the cream of the cream in the shire of the shires". He showed accordingly little enthusiasm when Lord Spencer asked him if he would pilot the

Empress of Austria. "What is an Empress to me? How can I look after her? I will do it of course but I would rather go my own way."

Word of his attitude reached Elizabeth and put her on her mettle. By the end of their first day together she had successfully proved to him that he should never have cause to complain that she had spoilt his fun. Encouraged by her, he rode his own line at his own pace and she followed him without hesitation. Few men would have done so after years of experience. It was Elizabeth's second day's hunting in Britain, and her first in the Shires. She was also his senior by nine years, and had been regarded for years as a partial invalid. The Pytchley country at that time took some crossing, being cattle country with big ditches to every fence and ox rails, or sometimes a double oxer.

It was all done with such style. There was no finer sight than "this perfect man to hounds followed by the best and most beautiful horsewoman that ever lived, their horses in perfect balance, taking each fence just as it came in a run." So thought Charles Kinsky, one of Elizabeth's Hungarian friends who later won the Grand National.

At last Elizabeth had found a way of life which used all her talents, her beauty, her charm, her horsemanship and her courage, and truly satisfied her. She revelled in the excitement and admiration, and enjoyed the company of close friends. She would give dinner parties after hunting where she was as relaxed and sparkling as she could be tense and preoccupied at some banquet in Vienna attended by important heads of state. With so little time at her disposal, she naturally missed few days. Her lady-in-waiting, bored and homesick, complained: "Other people hunt three or four times a week, but we seem to hunt every day."

She finished the season on a high note by arranging a special day's steeplechasing and presented a cup for the main race. This was known as the Hohenembs Cup after the name under which she was travelling incognita. Most appropriately it was won by Musketeer, owned and ridden by Captain Middleton.

Next autumn Bay was amongst the guests invited to Gödollo, as were a number of her English friends at different times, including Lord and Lady Spencer and later Lord Langford. Franz Joseph joined the party when possible, though his presence tended to turn every meal into a formal occasion. A true sportsman himself, he entertained his wife's guests with first class shooting and clearly found their company congenial. Despite all the rumours, he never seems to have regarded Bay as a rival, knowing how little the physical side of love meant to his wife. In this he was almost certainly right although he probably underestimated the strength of her emotions. On one occasion Bay, finding the entertainment at Gödollo not altogether adequate, decided to have a night out in Budapest. Elizabeth immediately arranged for a guide to show him round and was overcome with anxiety when the guide returned alone to report that the Englishman had vanished. She insisted on contacting the police. Unlike the Emperor, she was not amused when he eventually returned to confess that he had been robbed by a female acquaintance.

The next season the Russo-Turkish War prevented any possibility of a return to England, but at last at Christmas 1877 her plans were laid. In January she set off for London. That season she rented Cottesbrooke Park in the Pytchley country. In was a vintage time to be hunting in the Shires. Will Goodall was hunting the Pytchley, Tom Firr the Quorn, Frank Gillard the Belvoir and Mr. Tailby his own hounds. Elizabeth was better mounted than she had been for now the Austrian horses had been replaced with superb English hunters, personally selected, tried and if necessary schooled for her by Bay Middleton. The Empress, happy and at her healthiest with all the fresh air and exercise, looked as radiantly beautiful as ever. She wore an absolutely smooth chamois leather bodice under her habit into which she was sewn each day, and three pairs of gloves to protect her hands. Her perfectly cut habits showed off her elegant figure, but the lovely face was protected at every pause by a fan, not from the elements but from the curiosity of onlookers. This provoked the mockery of English ladies, jealous of her success and not subject to such unwanted attentions. Hunting as she did with so many different packs, she has left each with cherished memories of her. The prickly bullfinch fences round Burton Overy in Mr. Tailby's country made her warn her pilot, "Remember, I do not mind the falls but I will not scratch my face." The Warwickshire had an outstanding hunt from Shuckborough Hill that season: the presence of the Empress led to its commemoration in verse. Lord Willoughby de Broke, though, proved a less tolerant Master than Lord Spencer in the Pytchley country, who was used to the way his former A.D.C. and the

Empress overrode hounds. At the end of the Warwickshire day when Bay rode up to thank the Master he met with a sharp reply, "Damn you, Bay, you arrived an hour late and you've ridden over my hounds all day." Elizabeth intervened with her inimitable charm: "But you will forgive him for my sake." The Queen of Naples lacked this quality. Perhaps that is why Bay Middleton incurred her displeasure by responding to a request through the Embassy to pilot her in the absence of Elizabeth: "I'm damned if I'm going to pilot every damn Queen who comes to this country."

The season ended on an unfortunate note when Elizabeth's son Rudolf, also in England, pointedly refused to speak to Bay Middleton. When she heard, Elizabeth came close to a nervous breakdown, not hunting until the last day of her final week, and cheered only when Bay once more won the Hohenembs Cup at the Pytchley point-to-point next day. She formally thanked Will Goodall, giving him a jewelled pin, then immediately after the last race started the journey to Austria.

Bay had often told Elizabeth what a hunting paradise Ireland was. Despite the political complications, Franz Joseph, probably influenced by Spencer, sanctioned Elizabeth's plans and she arranged to take Summerhill in County Meath for the season of 1878–79. After a bad start to the season there was a prolonged freeze-up, and snow was still falling lightly when the Empress arrived on Saturday, 22nd February. The Irish gave Elizabeth a wonderful welcome, lighting bonfires and building arches over the roads, and she and Ireland fell in love with each other.

Tragically, no fewer than three of her horses had met with fatal accidents before her arrival, and Middleton advised the acquisition of some Irish horses. He also brought over his own Merry Andrew for her, who had carried her brilliantly in England, but then proved less successful steeplechasing. For her first day over banks with the Ward Union Staghounds the Master, Leonard Morrogh, mounted her on a superb brown blood horse named Domino. Despite nearly running away with her early on, he went so beautifully for her in a long fast hunt over a stiff line of country, when his owner, the Empress, Bay and Spencer had hounds to themselves, that Mr. Morrogh asked the Empress to accept him as a gift. He became probably her favourite hunter and Morrogh was honoured with becoming her pilot on a rare occasion when Bay was not

"The Empress Elizabeth of Austria with the Meath Hounds" April 1879. (*The B.B.C. Hulton Picture Library.*)

out. She went equally well on all her horses. She was not riding Domino when, smiling and unhesitating, she flew past Bay over a flooded brook as he turned away in search of a better place to jump. In eighteen days' hunting she had only one semblance of a fall, dismounting when her horse slipped up.

The most dramatic incident of her visit typified her approach throughout. After some fourteen miles as hounds ran, Bay, Spencer and the Empress jumped a wall close behind the Master to find themselves in the grounds of the college for Catholic priests at Maynooth. The Empress finished the day dressed in a warm cassock having lunch with the Rector. A few days later she returned, at her most bewitching, on a more formal visit. Catholic Ireland thrilled in response, Protestant England shuddered.

Her season ended abruptly when word came through of a flooding disaster in Hungary. Rising to the occasion as ever in such moments of national disaster, she returned home immediately. Later in the summer she celebrated her silver wedding.

Next February she came back to Summerhill. The season started inauspiciously. Domino was lamed on the first day when someone rode into him. Bay Middleton had too many horses in England to be able to mount himself properly also in Ireland and he had a succession of falls, but now she knew how to go on on her own. As a member of the field wrote in a song in her honour:

> "The best man in England can't lead her – he's down
> Bay Middleton's back is done beautifully brown. . . .
> He must ride who would follow
> The Queen of the Chase."

Soon Bay was back in his customary place. Domino was sound again and his mistress blissfully happy once more. Her contentment was short lived. The Irish political situation was deteriorating fast and word at last reached her from Franz Joseph that she must leave at once. She bade her last farewell to the island that came nearer to her island of dreams than any other.

There was no possibility of a return to Ireland. Instead she took Combermere Abbey in Cheshire for her next season. It was altered extensively to suit her: as usual the Emperor would have an astronomical bill to pay. But sadly the old magic had gone. She did not take the same pleasure in hunting in this type of country as she had done in Ireland and the Shires. Bay Middleton, marvellously recovered from a terrible fall on his head in the summer, did everything possible to brighten her, piloting her with his usual brilliance, even the day after concussing himself in another fall.

That summer of 1881 saw the wedding of Rudolf to Princess Stephanie of Belgium, an event which caused Elizabeth, perhaps more prescient than usual, deep depression. Anxious over this and disproportionately concerned by her increasing age and the impossibility of a return to Ireland, she came back to Cheshire. All hope for a reversion to her old spirit was gone when on arrival Bay announced the date of his marriage to Charlotte Baird. They had been unofficially engaged before he ever met the Empress: Elizabeth, unappreciative of Charlotte's tolerance and patience, regarded Bay's desertion as betrayal. She expressed total satisfaction with her new pilot, Major Rivers-Bulkeley, but showed little enthusiasm for hunting. There was a last brief flicker of the old delight when Bay, irresistibly drawn despite everything, "chanced" to hunt with the same hounds for two final days and Rivers-Bulkeley hastily stood down from his new post; then she brought the season to a premature close. Her farewell present to Bay was a beautifully jewelled miniature. Perhaps Charlotte Baird at least was pleased that the picture it contained was of the Emperor.

Elizabeth never hunted in England again. It could not be the same without Bay. Perhaps she felt that without him and with increasing age she would never go so well again and would gradually destroy that deservedly prized possession, her reputation. Perhaps indeed it would have been best if, as she wished at the time, she had broken her neck over a fence, as Bay himself was to do steeplechasing ten years later. Hunting to her was all part of her complex relationship with the man she probably loved more deeply than any other, even though the only physical expression of their love was in the hunting field.

The rest of Elizabeth's life was increasingly shadowed by despair and violence. Whilst she probably knew nothing of Bay Middleton's death, the tragic death of her mad but much loved cousin King Ludwig of Bavaria, followed by Rudolf's terrible suicide at Mayerling, made her own assassination in 1898 almost a relief. Deeply mourned by Franz Joseph ("No one will ever know how much I loved her" he murmured on hearing the news), perhaps otherwise those most saddened by the news were her English hunting friends. More than anyone else who knew her, they had most often seen the best side of her nature, charming everyone with a smile or confidence, a beautiful horsewoman with undaunted physical courage, delighting in the natural friendship and challenge of the hunting field. In return for the pleasure the sport gave her, she, quite unconsciously, changed the sport for her sex for ever. From then on no one could regard hunting as an eccentric, unconventional activity for a woman, even though this very feeling had contributed to its attraction for Elizabeth. Anything which an Empress did must be fashionable and desirable. Hunting for women had received the Imperial seal of approval.

# CHAPTER FIVE
# *FASHIONABLE AT LAST*

Throughout the 1870s and '80s the number of women in the hunting field increased dramatically. In 1877 Brooksby declared there were tenfold as many as twelve years before: perhaps thirty in a field of three hundred, although Guy Paget, who was not born until 1886, declared that when he was a boy in the Shires you could count on your fingers the women who hunted. There was also a change in attitude. Ladies increasingly came to regard it as fashionable to hunt. At first this merely meant that smart women who chose to hunt would not abstain from doing so for social reasons. Inevitably the pendulum gradually swung further: those who wished to be fashionable started to take up hunting.

Lady Augusta Fane first came to Melton in 1879. She was typical of the best of the female Meltonians. Smart, amusing, attractive, good company and very feminine, she also adored her hunting and, with her friends, was soon proving that, on the modern side saddles, women could ride across a country as well as men. She would rarely go home before the hounds, went out to dinner or dancing most evenings and hunted again next day. Whilst there would always be somebody to do her horses and clean her clothes, she did not have the convenience of a car or horse box. She would frequently have one and a half hours' hack at each end of the day's sport. An excellent horsewoman, she took the trouble to polish up her riding and give thought to the way she rode across a country. Above all, she watched hounds work. She much admired

"Lady Augusta Fane" 1894. From *Chit Chat* by Lady Augusta Fane

Tom Firr and fully appreciated that she was hunting with perhaps the greatest huntsman of all time.

Firr was disappointed when she did not invite him to take part in the "Moonlight Steeplechase" held to celebrate her birthday. Captain Warner, the Master, had asked her not to include him in case Firr was injured, and it was fortunate that no-one was damaged in the escapade. Whilst the idea originated with Lady Augusta, all the eleven competitors were men. After a dinner party they lined up at 11.30 p.m., white nightshirts over their red tail coats, the fences marked by lamps on each side but the moon unfortunately hidden by clouds. Three horses fell but no damage was done, though the local parson, inexplicably shocked, rebuked them from the pulpit next Sunday.

Amongst those to enjoy hunting in Leicestershire at this time was Margot Tennant, before her marriage to the future Prime Minister Herbert Henry Asquith. Not a great horsewoman, despite her avowal that, "I had a genius for horses and adored hunting", she made up in pluck for what she lacked in skill and soon had many young men attempting to follow her over the fences. She cheerfully informed them that they "looked like a string of onions trailing after me!" But then, as "Dick Heathen" in Guy Paget's *Rum 'Uns to Follow* said of her: "She was never the first class – too full of talk ever to be a real foxhunter." She records in her *Autobiography* (dubbed by Lady Augusta "The Importance of Being Margot") that she had never jumped a fence before her first day's hunting, when, not surprisingly, she fell off the first time her horse left the ground. Unabashed, she bore witness to "the perfect certainty I had that I would ride better than anyone in the whole world."

Amusingly as she tells of her escapades, she cannot always have endeared herself to those concerned. When her own hireling did not appear at the meet, she persuaded a horseman to hand over to her a second horse belonging to someone she had never met. Nor was her father amused when she rode her hack up the steps through the front door of their London house into the hall. The horse caught sight of itself in a mirror, panicked and came down, causing considerable damage.

So, as with the men fifty years earlier, the true lovers of venery were soon heavily outnumbered by those interested in the fun, the social side and the ride across country, but not in hounds. Yet this has always been the case with almost any hunting field in any good riding country. The pundits of the time were perhaps hard in levelling this charge against the women in particular. Otho Paget declared that there were "any number of women whom I have had the pleasure of seeing ride brilliantly across Leicestershire, and many of them first-rate riders, but very few who could keep their eyes on hounds and at the same time take their own line". He excepts only the Duchess of Hamilton, Mrs. Bunbury and, with reservations, Lady Gerard. Proportionately the men were probably no better. Others went further and criticised not only the attention to hounds but the horsemanship: "Not to put too fine a point on it, the majority of horsewomen ride abominably", wrote S. Sidney in 1875.

The increasing numbers of women in the field certainly began to attract a barrage of criticism, some of which must have been justified. Women were accused of bad manners, riding too close to the man in front, undue pushing and selfish behaviour. "Horse dealers, farmers and – we are sorry to add – ladies, must especially be avoided: for whoever saw a vicious kicker that was not ridden by one of these?" wrote Brooksby. One man told a lady that she was the forty-second lady he had held a gate for, and the first who had said "Thank you". One hunt secretary went further: "The ordinary hunting woman would no more dream of riding up a furrow to save the rest of the field than she would dream of flying, and she will revel in a gallop over a turnip-field, ignoring the fact that a turnip dies at every stride of her horse. She rarely knows seeds from old grass land, and if she did I fear I am not convinced that she would turn her mount a hair's breadth out of the way."

Whether or not women took less interest in hounds than men, undoubtedly a number of women at this time did display ignorance and lack of consideration in the field. There were several reasons for this. Unlike their brothers, most women had not been brought up with the expectation of hunting: the principles which had been drummed into the schoolboy sons of sporting families had not been mentioned to daughters. Many had had little chance to improve their horsemanship: there was no Pony Club and, outside big towns, few riding schools where ladies could be taught to jump.

Then the very novelty of their position seems too frequently to have engendered undesirable reactions. Either they became excessively cocky: "Oh, thank you, we don't ride like that, it's quite out of date", one young lady rebuked an experienced adviser who suggested she should shorten her stirrup. She finished the day with a broken collar-bone, for an unduly long leather, whilst looking smart, gives an insecure seat on a side saddle. Or else they were overcome with nerves. This, as is frequently demonstrated out hunting, can lead to displays of rudeness and bad temper which would horrify the offender when safely on the ground.

Flirtations out hunting caused some amusement. "Cubhunting as usual?" queried a Master passing a female member of his field surrounded by a group of admiring boys.

The position of women in the field at this time was somewhat ambiguous. On the one hand they were accorded certain privileges. Before 1891 ladies were not asked to subscribe: two years later the Leicestershire hunts agreed they would ask them to pay a cap. As late as 1920 a few packs had a lower subscription rate for ladies, despite one (male) secretary's comment that they did three times as much damage. They were at first given priority at

"Hunting Scene" by George Wright. (*Courtesy of Richard Green Galleries, London.*)

gates and gaps and remained unrebuked for behaviour forbidden to men. Perhaps this early lenient treatment encouraged the bad behaviour which was soon so widely commented on.

On the other hand the feminine role was deemed a passive one. In a book published in 1894, Mrs. Chaworth Musters took considerable exception to women taking "an active part in field management, like the well-meaning dame who is reported to have said to an offender, 'If I were a gentleman I would swear at you'." That lady, she felt, had let "zeal outrun discretion".

Equally shocking to contemporary opinion, which in this case has stood the test of time, were occasional attempts at dressing like men. In 1886 a group of well-known ladies with the Cottesmore planned to appear in scarlet jackets at the same meet. The scheme was not a success. Mrs. Sam Garnett tried a similar outfit when she first came to the Shires from Ireland, but despite its superb cut and her admirable figure she met with general disapproval and no imitators.

Other modifications proved more acceptable. Proper hunting whips were now carried by women as well as men, enabling them to be more independent at gates. Safety skirts also were no longer frowned on: indeed the Quorn issued an ultimatum in 1884 that women must wear a safety skirt or give up riding to hounds.

One lady hunting in the late 1870s who would have liked to see considerable changes in women's dress and in other directions was that early and ardent feminist Lady Florence Caroline Dixie. Amongst the many causes which she espoused whole-heartedly was that of rational dress for women. She had her hair cut like a boy's and would appear clad in a white flannel blouse, a tartan kilt just covering her knees and long tartan stockings, revolutionary dress indeed for the time. She was one of the earliest supporters of women riding cross saddle, and once rode bareback into the Post Office in Melton Mowbray, completed her business and left without dismounting.

Lady Florence is a figure much more in tune with the 1980s than the 1880s: her feminist views were described by *The Times* in her obituary in 1905 as "somewhat peculiar, going far beyond those of other supporters of Women's Rights". She actually contended that all occupations and professions should be equally open to both sexes, and that there should be absolute equality in marriage, divorce and inheritance laws, and in relation to titles.

A daughter of the seventh Marquess of Queensberry, in her younger days she was a great sportswoman. She revelled in going where others hesitated to follow, whether it was a journey to Patagonia, or crossing an impossibly flood-swollen river in the hunting field, glorying, as she stood dripping on the further side after her inevitable soaking, in having "pounded" the whole field. She was one of the first women to travel to far countries in search of big game: she had killed lions in Africa, stalked gazelles in Arabia and bears in the Rocky Mountains. She and her husband Sir Alexander Dixie were nicknamed Sir Always and Lady Sometimes Tipsy. At one stage she kept a jaguar cub, brought back from her travels, at her hunting box.

But then a complete change came over her: she turned against hunting, publishing a pamphlet entitled "The Horrors of Sport" and declared: "I whom some have called a female Nimrod have come to regard with absolute loathing and detestation any sort or kind of sport which is produced by the sufferings of animals." From then on her excitements came from dangerous exploits in remote places and the advocacy of all she believed in. She persuaded the *Morning Post* to appoint her its war correspondent for the First Boer War, sending back thrilling despatches, and later claiming that it was through her advocacy that Cetewayo, the captured king of Zululand, was restored to liberty and sent back to his homeland.

Another female war correspondent conspicuous in the hunting field was Lord Randolph Churchill's sister Lady Sarah Wilson. She was with her husband, who was A.D.C. to Baden-Powell, throughout the siege of Mafeking, was taken prisoner by the Boers and later exchanged.

The most eccentric of all those hunting in the latter part of the 19th century was almost certainly Lady Cardigan. Born Adeline de Horsey, she first met Lord Cardigan, the controversial hero of the charge of the Light Brigade, on his return from the Crimean War and, as he had long been separated from his first wife, went to live with him in London. She thus precluded herself for the rest of her life from acceptance in court circles. She became Lady Cardigan on the death of her predecessor, but was relatively soon left a widow with a life interest in his fortune and home of Deene Park in Northamptonshire.

A remarkable-looking woman, she was also well educated,

spoke five languages and showed great musical talent. Yet her efforts to retain the appearance and outlook of a girl of seventeen throughout the ninety-two years of her life made her an increasingly farcical figure. But nothing delighted her more than to attract attention, and if this was what the excessive powder and rouge, the wig of golden curls and the extraordinary clothes achieved, she was well satisfied.

She hunted sometimes from Deene, sometimes from her hunting box at Melton. Yet she never really enjoyed hunting and would continue her games of make-believe by sending her horses home then driving about asking if anyone had seen them, and abusing the groom for taking them to the wrong place. She continued this pretence years after she had given up hunting, driving to the meet in her habit. Dressing up was one of life's many pleasures for her: visitors to Deene sometimes found her arrayed in Lord Cardigan's military uniform, dressed as a Spanish dancer or even pretending to be the ghost of a Grey Nun. In her later years she had her coffin installed in the hall and periodically climbed into it, arrayed in a blue silk dress.

Before she acquired her magnificent wig, her hair still gleamed a glorious gold. She once arrived at Melton, and, when her belongings were unpacked, hastily despatched a groom back to Deene to fetch what she described as a bottle of medicine which had been left behind. Unfortunately the bottle, which was fastened to the horse on the offside while the groom was fetching it, leaked. Next day she appeared at the meet on the same horse and, having mounted on the nearside, did not notice the offside. There was universal delight at finding a large portion of the horse's dark coat lightened to a glossy pinkish gold.

Such characters, whilst enlivening life, did little for the serious female reputation in the hunting field. Many women showed remarkable keenness: Daisy, the future Countess of Warwick, hunted three days a week but had to slip quietly away in order to escape the disapproving eye of her father-in-law. A few took the trouble to learn enough about the science of hunting as well as of horsemanship to be a positive asset in the field rather than the tiresome and often dangerous liability so many of the newcomers were proving themselves. Most of the wiser ones had the benefit of the counsel of experienced hunting men behind them: on her first arrival in Melton Lady Augusta Fane was fortunate

"The York and Ainsty Hounds on the Ferry at Newby" by Thomas Blinks. 1898. From *Sporting Art: England 1700–1900* by Stella A. Walker, (*Courtesy of Mrs. Walker.*)

enough to stay with Lord and Lady Grey de Wilton. But understanding of problems often comes only with the assumption of responsibility. Women's right to appear in the hunting field was undisputed by the turn of the century. "No one would dream nowadays of treating the question of whether women should hunt at all as an open one," wrote T.F. Dale in 1903. "The only discussion that ever arises is whether women should hunt four days or six in a week." What was not open to women except in unusual circumstances was to take on any form of responsibility. Lady Yarborough, after her husband's death and during her son's minority, took on the Brocklesby Hounds, the family pack, just as she assumed responsibility for the management of the estate. She proved an admirable Master, and is the third woman, following Lady Salisbury in the 18th century and Mrs. Ingram mentioned below, to be recognised as a Master by the Masters of Foxhounds Association.

In 1871 Hugo Francis Meynell Ingram, Master of the Hoar Cross Hounds, which subsequently became the Meynell, died. He had succeeded his father in the Mastership, his father having founded the country. The Master's widow therefore defrayed the cost of hunting the country for the 1871–72 season, before giving the hounds to the country. But the first women Masters of Foxhounds in a modern sense did not take office until the 20th century.

The same step was taken a decade earlier in the world of harriers and beagles. Most women who were really interested in hunting at this time favoured harehounds rather than foxhounds. Perhaps they felt there was less prejudice against them. But harriers and beagles have always had a particular appeal for true lovers of hunting. More likely the prejudice evaporated as knowledgeable women gradually moved into positions of responsibility, paving the way for a similar development in the foxhound world. "Ladies", wrote G.F. Underhill in 1903, are "absolutely in place with otterhounds, and they nowhere show to more advantage than beside the water in the blue, red or green of the hunt uniform." This author was surprised when a lady volunteered to turn hounds as they were seen running fast into the distance, and impressed when she did so. His amazement was unbounded when he learnt that she had cycled seventy miles on the previous day to enable her to hunt. H.H. Bryden in the same year expressed astonishment at the way ladies in his day would "brave weather, mud, hill, ploughing and other obstacles in their determination to see sport".

Perhaps women were more easily accepted in the beagling world in that earlier in the 19th century the slow, heavy beagles then popular had been considered "admirably adapted for ladies and gentlemen up in years. . . . (There were) few male persons of any activity that could not keep up with them." What was remarkable was that as the beagles became faster, so did the ladies.

One of the first to take office as Master was the famous and much loved Mrs. Cheape, known as the Squire of Bentley. Maude Mary Hemming was born in 1853. Her father, Richard Hemming, owned a six thousand acre estate at Bentley in Worcestershire to which he devoted his life, running it in the best traditions of the old-fashioned squire. His first concern was always the welfare of his tenants, employees and their families, who in turn gave him their devotion and absolute trust. A kind, generous man and great sportsman, his principles were upheld in full at Bentley and elsewhere by his daughter Maude Cheape.

As a child, she was generally encouraged in her love of riding and hunting by her father, although he seems sometimes to have had reservations about her activities, perhaps fearing for her safety. She showed a natural ability and fearlessness on a horse which far outstripped her brother or sisters. A keen reader, she enjoyed both music and painting all her life, but horrified her French governess by her refusal to wear crinolines. What she liked best was to be with her ponies and dogs, performing circus tricks, riding bareback or bringing ponies into the house.

She soon charmed a neighbour, Squire Haywood, into encouraging her hunting and often providing a mount for her if she encountered parental resistance. Her diary, written at the age of ten, tells of "some capital jumping, a lot of rails and a very awkward leap over a drop through a willow tree amongst them". Rather later, it mentions trying to "fall in with hounds" by accident, having jumped numerous fences to get there, and of the anxiety of sudden meetings with Papa. He in fact adored her, declaring her longing for the chase to be inherited from him, and generally allowed her to stay with hounds. She was soon a determined as well as an elegant horsewoman, persisting with the most difficult horses until she had them going as they should. She started to ride and school a large selection of young horses, in itself an unusual thing for a woman of the time to do.

She was her father's companion in much that he did, learning from him about the Bentley estate and about pictures (he had a fine collection, notably of Landseers) as well as about sport. Much of each summer was spent on their Scottish estate of Glaschorrie. When her only brother showed an unfortunate predilection for gambling, her father resolved to make Maude his heir in her brother's place. In the event, her brother predeceased their father.

Notwithstanding the dashing way she rode to hounds, her worst riding accident happened when she was eighteen in what she called "the gilded cage" of London. Her horse slipped up, she hit her head and was unconscious for some hours. At her "coming out" ball she opened the dancing with the eminent physician who had attended her, her head still bandaged. Passing the scene of the accident a short time afterwards, she heard two old ladies talking:

"Yes, this is just where it happened. That lovely young thing, only eighteen, and killed on the spot!" She was able to reassure them.

In the same year, she became engaged to Lt.-Col. George Clerk Cheape, despite parental reservations, largely on account of her age. Colonel Cheape shared his wife's sporting interests and, after a honeymoon in his home country of Scotland, fishing and hunting hill foxes with three couple of old hounds, they settled north of the border. Mrs. Cheape was soon as well loved in Fife as she was at Bentley. An outstandingly good-looking woman, Mr. Fairfax-Blakeborough described her after her death as the antithesis of the non-sporting image of a sportswoman: "All the culture and refinement of life were hers." Kind, sympathetic, generous and feminine, she showed also qualities then regarded as masculine in her ability to deal with all the problems that came her way, whether they concerned estate management, hounds, horses, sports or agriculture. Everything that she did was done efficiently and with style. When she organised a goat show during her first year in Scotland, all the goats were equipped with rugs like those worn by horses, edged in red.

In 1875 Katie, the first of her six children, was born. Mrs. Cheape proved herself over the years as fine a mother as she was a sportswoman.

In 1877 her husband took on the Mastership of the West Fife country, under Colonel Anstruther Thomson, who retained the nominal Mastership of the whole Fife country. Maude was soon known as the A.D.C. or Aide de Chasse, a job she did admirably and enjoyed enormously, being very sad when someone else took over her husband's office for one season. Colonel Cheape spent much time in America where he had considerable, though unsuccessful, business interests, and his wife fulfilled his responsibilities in his absence. She was a remarkably energetic person, who thought nothing of walking over to visit a friend, a round trip of twenty-four miles. She also excelled in her relations with people of every kind, always taking the infinite trouble which amounts to genius. If a misunderstanding arose between her husband and the professional huntsman, she would make peace. When a whipper-in was required, she trained a post boy from Mull to make a first-class one. She was not only an outstanding horsewoman but had an eye for a horse which enabled her to buy anything

"The Squire of Bentley (Mrs. Cheape) with her pack in 1891" from *The Squire of Bentley* by Maudie A. Ellis.

from a London cab horse to a Highland pony and make it into an excellent hunter. She was eventually persuaded to sell one favourite mare to a friend as a London hack for £150. She was later horrified to learn that the hack's new owner had decided she was unrideable and sent her to an auction sale. Mrs. Cheape took considerable trouble to trace the mare to a suburban riding school, eventually buying her back for £30. The mare proved a great hunter, won in the show ring and subsequently bred several point-to-point winners. Mrs. Cheape was always ready to learn, going after the birth of her youngest child to the riding school at Knightsbridge Barracks for a complete military training riding course.

In 1887 Colonel Cheape took the Linlithgow and Stirling Hounds, and he and his wife stayed in that country until 1890. In 1890 Mrs. Cheape started her own pack of beagles, which she hunted herself, the Wellfield Beagles. This was partly for the benefit of the children, whose education in certain directions she attended to personally. They were brought up to spend much time out of doors, going hunting with their mother. She tried to teach them not only about the sport but about the broader principles of life in which she so firmly believed. Consideration for others, thoughtfulness, self reliance and determination were amongst the virtues she taught them to show in the context of the hunting field and apply throughout their lives. Sometimes they rode their ponies with the beagles, and indeed their mother hunted hounds mounted. Occasionally they were expected to run, to give them practical experience of a pony's feelings when asked to cross a heavy plough too fast. The children also were involved in every aspect of kennel life. Mounted paper chases helped them to understand a hound's problems in working out a line. Boys and girls participated equally, the girls riding cross saddle until they were twelve or fourteen, a revolutionary idea at the time, but a wise one. As they became old enough they whipped-in to their mother.

By then they were living in Worcestershire once more. In 1890 Richard Hemming, the old Squire, became ill and his daughter spent much time in London with him, bringing with her four couple of beagles. By way of relaxation she and a groom would take them early in the morning to Hyde Park, where the groom would lay a drag for them to hunt. The next year her father died, leaving her heir to Bentley and Glaschorrie: a mammoth inheritance, but an equally large responsibility, an aspect she never ignored. The estate workmen at Bentley started calling her the Squire of Bentley. Agriculture and the welfare of her tenants and employees now absorbed as much of her time and energy as her children and sport. She was soon involved in breeding cattle, sheep and horses and installing electricity at Bentley.

She was deeply loved in Worcestershire, if her methods sometimes caused astonishment. A jubilant keeper, hauling two poachers before her, was disappointed when she gave each a shilling and a packet of tobacco, bidding them not to do it again, yet remarkably there was no poaching on the estate for years afterwards. Another keeper, a new man named Cox, was warned, "Remember, no fox, no Cox."

No good cause lacked support from her and no individual need was neglected. An old servant wrote:

> "Should there be anyone ill – man, woman or child – and she knew it, she would see they were well looked after, not a drop of soup today and then forgotten, but whatever was wanted until they were well, and coals to keep the home fires burning if it was needed. So who can forget such a noble-hearted mistress, and I feel sure all those who served under her will bear me out in this."

She always longed to help everyone. On hearing how a horse, which subsequently won the Derby, had got loose and the young lad blamed had been forbidden to ride in future, she wondered if she could help by giving him a job with hunters.

"No, Squire," she was told, "no lad who has ever been in a racing stable will be contented out of it." The young lad's name was Steve Donoghue.

The beagles were soon joined by a pack of harriers, for the family were growing up, and all loved horses as much as hounds. This pack, the Bentley Harriers, achieved remarkable success in the field and on the flags. The Squire collected and bred them with her usual flair and attention to detail and in the late 1890s they won a remarkable number of prizes at Peterborough. Particularly outstanding was Bentley Wellfield, who won the championship in 1895. They were often invited away from home to hunt, spending some weeks for several successive seasons in Berkshire. They also periodically showed sport to all the Squire's old friends north of the border. In 1900 she took on a second pack of harriers on the death of their Master, but they were kennelled thirty-two miles from Bentley and after two seasons she found the strain too great and sold them. Later she acquired some deer for carted deer hunting. She sometimes took some of the family to the New Forest in the spring to hunt, together with horses and ponies, but not, in this case, hounds.

"A Good Pilot" by George Wright. (*Courtesy of Richard Green Galleries, London.*)

Much of the summer was spent on Mull, her husband's Highland estate, to keep which she had reluctantly had to sell Glaschorrie. She welcomed to the island all her friends, be they retired hunt servants, Bentley tenants or Masters of Foxhounds, paying their travelling expenses where appropriate and giving them a marvellous holiday, whether they sought stalking (deer and goat), fishing, sailing, rowing, musical evenings, landscapes to paint or just a well-earned rest.

In Mull in 1896 the first tragedy of the Squire's life occurred. Her twelve-year-old daughter Daisy, a sunny-natured, bright child who rode beautifully and fearlessly and accompanied her mother everywhere, was drowned in a sailing accident. The Squire never really recovered her joy in living, though characteristically she struggled to appear unchanged for the sake of those around her.

However, the beagles, which had been a particular interest of Daisy's, were then sold. She showed this resilience all her life. When a favourite horse broke a leg when ridden by a friend, she was the one who consoled the borrower.

In 1905 she had a fall on her feet, breaking her thigh in two places. Despite long months in bed and being unable to ride for two years, she was never bored but busy painting and writing. Her oldest son Hugh hunted hounds for her, but when he moved to Berwickshire in 1908 she finally sold her harriers, going back to beagles. Soon after this she gave up riding.

From 1914 the clouds gathered with increasing fury over her as over so many others. In that year her eldest daughter Katie was drowned when the ship the *Empress of Ireland* went down. The beagles had to go on the outbreak of war. In 1916 her son Leslie, one of the outstanding polo players of his time, if not the foremost, was killed fighting. In 1918 her oldest son Hugh was drowned when the ship carrying the regiment he commanded was torpedoed. Only two of her six adored, happy and successful children were left, Ronald, by then a Brigadier General, and Maudie Ellis, her mother's biographer. Maudie herself became in 1923 the first woman to ride two winners in a single day, at the Linlithgow and Stirling point-to-point. She inherited many of her mother's finest characteristics.

In 1918 the war, which in so many places had passed the responsibility for hunting from men to women, was over. But the Squire of Bentley's world was shattered beyond repair, and in 1919 she died.

Another great early Master of Harriers was Miss Isa McClintock, who took on the Tynan and Armagh in Ireland in 1899 having been unanimously elected on the resignation of the previous Master. For many years she was re-elected annually, hunting hounds herself for some thirty years, and reviving the country after an interval during the First World War despite having such limited funds that she was forced to have the pack trencher fed. She remained Master until her death in September 1952, when she was in her eighty-eighth year. She managed to ride to her last Boxing Day meet in 1951.

Perhaps the two other most outstanding lady Masters around the turn of the century were Mrs. (subsequently Dame Margaret) Pryse Rice and Lady Gifford. The former established her pack of harriers in South Wales in 1894 when her husband gave up his foxhounds. Although technically harriers, they hunted both hare and fox, in rough moor and woodland country, with the Master hunting hounds herself. Her daughter and the kennel huntsman whipped-in to her. Mrs. Pryse Rice was amongst the very few ladies at this time to hunt her own hounds, and continued to do so for twenty-five years. They were a smart looking pack, often successful at Peterborough. After her first two seasons she increased the size of hound from eighteen inches to twenty inches, finding that they could cope better with the country, the long distances and perhaps also with the foxes.

Lady Gifford established her harriers a season after Mrs. Pryse Rice, and also hunted them herself. For the first three seasons they were in Northumberland: in 1898 she moved with the pack to Sussex. The Gifford family were a hunting family: old Lord Gifford is sometimes said to have been the original of Surtees' character Lord Scamperdale.

So by the turn of the century women were established as Masters, sometimes hunting hounds themselves, with the beagle and harrier packs. Their reputation for irresponsibility in the foxhound world was soon to fade as here too they proved successful in positions of authority.

# CHAPTER SIX
# *SHOULDERING RESPONSIBILITIES*

The early 20th century brought women into positions of responsibility with foxhounds as well as harriers. Many of the women were either succeeding or joining their husbands, fathers or brothers in the Mastership, but this in no way detracts from their performance. A number of packs at the time tended to draw their Masters from one or perhaps two families, and in some cases the female Master proved a more powerful personality than her male predecessor or colleague; her very willingness to accept the position indicated considerable force of character.

The first of these women was Mrs. T.H.R. Hughes, who became Master of the Neuadd Fawr in Carmarthen and Cardigan in Wales in 1902 and retained that position for twenty-five seasons. She had been brought up to hunt, going out with harriers from the age of six and later hunting with the Oakley. She married for the first time in 1895 but her husband died three years later. She then married T.H.R. Hughes in 1899, who had started the Neuadd Fawr Hounds in 1876 and been Master ever since. When he also died after just three years of marriage, in September 1902, she took on the hounds with great success. The hounds were a private pack. She had no guarantee, nor did she take subscriptions or caps.

A keen gardener and farmer, Mrs. Hughes was also a successful breeder of hunters, shorthorn cattle and Shropshire sheep. She also set the fashion in other ways, declaring in 1910 that whilst she had hitherto followed the usual custom of riding on a side

"Mrs. T.H.R. Hughes riding astride" From *British Hunts and Huntsmen.*

saddle, she intended in future to hunt astride. An interesting picture shows her mounted. At first glance she appears to the casual observer to be side saddle. Closer inspection reveals that she is in fact astride, but so dressed that the distinction is hard to detect. Her coat is long, as was the custom at the time, and she is wearing a skirt, even though she is astride, and a top hat, not a master's hunting cap. Top hats for ladies at the time were less widespread than they became after the First World War, many women preferring the bowler.

Mrs. Hughes, as sole Master of a private pack of hounds, was able to change to the cross saddle without opposition when persuaded of its advantages. She must already have done a considerable amount of riding astride, perhaps as a child, to be able to adapt so easily. For others, different problems arose, apart from their personal comfort and convenience.

In much of the hunting world the idea of women riding astride was greeted with outrage. It was deemed to be unattractive and unfeminine. Lord Annaly, Master of the Pytchley from 1902 to 1914, was particularly outspoken in his disapproval of the practice and went so far as to refuse to give the Pytchley white collar to any woman who rode astride. He was no doubt old-fashioned and reactionary. He was also a great admirer of smart and correct turnout: women did, and do, look more attractive correctly turned out side saddle than they ever can astride.

Whilst little thought was given at the time to the relative safety of the two methods of riding, there were some serious accidents to women. These received excessive comment because women were involved, though, as one husband remarked when his wife made a good recovery after being dragged and kicked in the face, "They take a lot of killing, women do!" Lady Harrington lost the sight of one eye following a bad fall on the head. She rode in point-to-points despite the accident and had another fall on the head. She proved remarkably lucky: on opening her eyes she found that the second fall had restored the sight to her damaged eye.

Women hunted with worse disabilities than the loss of sight in one eye. One hunted with the Pytchley even though she had been born without hands and Lady Downshire lost a leg but continued to go remarkably well to hounds.

A few side saddles were made with the pommels on the offside rather than the nearside, which could be useful in case of a temporary minor disability. Such saddles were preferred by some ladies who found them more comfortable, amongst them Queen Alexandra, who hunted regularly with the West Norfolk, often on such

---

*Opposite* "Alexandra, Princess of Wales on Viva at Sandringham, showing the right handed side saddle which is still in the Royal Mews" by Lacretelle. (*Reproduced by Gracious Permission of Her Majesty the Queen.*)

a saddle.

A year after Mrs. Hughes, in 1903, another, more famous, woman added the letters M.F.H. to her name. Edith Somerville is better remembered for her share in the writing partnership of Somerville and Ross, creators of the Irish R.M. The first volume of these delightful stories, *Experiences of an Irish R.M.*, was published four years before Miss Somerville took on the Mastership of the West Carbery Hounds in County Cork in Ireland.

Edith Somerville was born in 1858. Her grandfather had once had the West Carbery Hounds. When she was four he placed her, bundled in a rug, on the back of a cob no older than herself, and let go of the reins. Their fall, entangled in the ropes of a garden swing, caused remarkably little damage, physical or psychological. A year later, dressed in a long full skirt and miniature top hat on a more suitable pony but using a "deformed and deforming little saddle", her rides with the old man chanced increasingly frequently to bring them out with hounds. On one glorious occasion the brush was presented to Edith. All this was done surreptitiously, for the old man's doctor and the women of the household discouraged hunting, though it was eventually ended by the temporary demise of the West Carbery. Edith thereafter had to go visiting for her hunting. Her horsemanship so improved that a knowledgeable old horse breaker friend paid her a compliment she valued all her life: "'Twas the Grandfather gave you the sate, but 'twas the Lord Almighty that gave you the hands!"

Life in such an Irish country house as the Somerville family home of Drishane in Victorian times was not calculated to make a fragile flower of a girl, despite female reservations about her early hunting. Indeed, whilst her mother did not hunt, her grandmother many years before reached the turning point in her life in the hunting field. The grandmother and her sister in their youth, both equally attractive and at that time close friends, fell in love with the same young man. The sister, when both were hunting, came back to find the young man devotedly attending her rival, who had had a bad fall. Not only did the young man become Edith's grandfather, but the sisters remained unreconciled for the rest of their long lives.

Edith's own childhood was filled with horses and dogs, perilous climbs on steep cliffs, adventures with boats and guns, and all the other excitements of an untrammelled country life with five brothers and a sister. She also helped her mother in local attempts to alleviate some part of the appalling poverty and starvation then afflicting much of Ireland. The artistic side of her nature was developed in music, writing and, at first predominantly, painting, which she studied seriously in London, Germany and, most successfully, Paris.

When Edith was thirty-three, her brother Aylmer revived the West Carbery by buying a small pack of hounds known as "B's Rioters". He started to hunt the country, with his sister's help, in as wild and light-hearted a manner as ever a pack of hounds was hunted, even in Ireland. They revelled in the fun of it, caring nothing for decorum and correctness, and were well liked by most of the local people. Their methods would not have earned the approval of the Masters of Foxhounds Association. The country was not well, or evenly, foxed, so traps were set and foxes thus caught released as bagmen. Some of Aylmer's local popularity may be attributed to his willingness to pay ten shillings a fox. Edith's diary entry for 26th December narrates one capture: "They swam after him to an island and hunted him naked round and round until he lay down and was caught." Failing the great, wolf-like West Carbery foxes, which later embarrassed Edith by causing her to mistake the masks around the walls of a fashionable English kennel for cubs, hounds made do with hunting sheep, cur-dogs or cats.

Another diary entry recounts the arrival of a man with a fox for sale. During a row over the price, a guest was "knocked down and walked on by the mule that drew the cart, that held the barrel, that held the fox, which in the melee escaped". Edith's diary on another occasion summarizes the sport thus: "Mixed bag. Killed a fox, a rabbit, a goat and a woodcock. The latter buzzed into Crowley's face out of a furze bush, and he hit it down with the horn."

The country also was a rough and wild one, where the best sort of mount was generally considered to be a weight-carrying goat. Fences could be walls, banks or bedsteads. Fields might average twenty people. The whipper-in, Martin Ross recorded, was dressed in "a greasy tweed cap, torn brown gaiters and an old pink coat of so voluminous a cut as to suggest a divided skirt, and also – which was perhaps as well – to enfold in mystery the nature of his breeches."

A heavy share of the organisation fell on Edith's capable shoulders. Aylmer was no businessman and even the most chaotic of hunting establishments requires much work to keep it in existence. Certainly she was at her brother's side in the worst crisis of his regime. In August 1897 the pack contracted rabies. None could be saved, and Aylmer and Edith set out to find the most swift and merciful poison possible, leaving two policemen with rifles at the kennels. In their absence two hounds became raging mad, and the Kennel Huntsman was forced to drag out hound after hound, at considerable risk to himself, and shoot them all. Brother and sister returned to the appalling sight of the whole pack, whom they had bred, hunted and loved, lying dead. Through the kindness and generosity of Masters of Hounds throughout Britain, they were able to collect a new pack of hounds, which was established in new kennels built by the Master's father before the end of September.

Edith Somerville was a remarkably forceful character, her personality overpowering her five brothers, none of whom was in the least weak or ineffectual, in an age when many women would have taken a subordinate position for granted. Edith, on the contrary, became an active feminist, presiding over the Munster Women's Franchise League. Whilst she was most artistic, she was not a feminine creature, causing her mother to deplore her appearance, describing her as "the Disgrace of Castle Townshend"! More than this, her instincts were basically homosexual, although, in the words of her biographer Maurice Collis, the emotion "did not include what she would have termed its grosser manifestations". When she was twenty-one and her best friend announced her engagement, Edith's reactions were of shock, horror, disapproval and revulsion.

Seven years later she met the woman who was to fill both the emotional and the artistic void in her life. Violet Martin was four years younger than Edith, a second cousin, who had spent the first decade of her life at Ross, her family home, in the County of Galway, leading a similar life to Edith (though Ross was more remote and less anglicised than Drishane) before her father's death precipitated a move to Dublin. In her mid-twenties she returned to Ross with her mother, a lady who, though the authors denied any resemblance, had much in common with the superb Mrs. Knox of the R.M. stories, just as many of the problems which

"Edith Somerville, creator of the Irish R.M." From *British Hunts and Huntsmen*.

beset them in restoring Ross were later allotted to Major and Mrs. Yeates.

There was another Violet in Edith's circle of friends and cousins, so her new friend came to be called Martin Ross. Martin was a sensitive, gentle girl with a rare literary talent and a bubbling sense of humour. She found in her collaborator and friend the perfect foil for her genius. Edith in her turn realised that her own true potential lay in the field of literature, not art. Their first book, *An Irish Cousin*, was published in 1889, to the surprise of Edith's family, who had laughed throughout its creation at "that nonsense of the girls'", and nicknamed the book "The Shocker". The method of collaboration has caused astonishment ever since: each point was discussed, then committed to paper by whoever happened to be holding the pen, with remarkable success.

By the time Miss Somerville took on the Mastership, they had published some ten books. Edith continued her painting and playing the organ, kept up an extensive correspondence, was much involved with stables, kennels and her own dogs and, largest commitment of all, since the deaths of her parents had become mistress of the enormous, rat-infested family home of Drishane on behalf of herself and her brothers, a problem rendered the more difficult by a chronic shortage of money.

A professional huntsman was now employed, though the Master sometimes hunted hounds herself. The professional was often an Englishman which, as Martin wrote, "adds to his mystery, and, in a certain unconfessed sense, to his greatness. He does not, as a rule, understand what they are saying; he does not even wish to do so, which, in itself, is impressive." The Master herself spent much time in kennels and was knowledgeable about hounds, though her levity occasionally shocked the huntsman, as when she proposed using a couple of hounds with the fourteen family dogs in a drag hunt. "Oh, Master, you wouldn't ask them pore 'ounds to do such a thing?"

Practical jokes were also popular. In reprisal for a previous episode, they once removed a horse from a neighbour's stable on the eve of April Fool's Day. Next day when he recovered it he found every rib on its thin body delineated in red paint, his initials on its quarters, zebra stripes on its neck and spectacles round its eyes.

Being a Master of Hounds involves quite as much hard work as amusement. Miss Somerville had taken on the position when her brother moved to England fully aware of the problems with which she would have to grapple. Amongst her worst headaches were the ever-present one of finance and the difficulties of administering the Fowl Fund. At this time hunts expected to pay compensation for all poultry taken by foxes. The resulting problems in assessing appropriate compensation were endless and caused extensive correspondence such as this:

"Dear Miss, just a few lines to let you know the fox is making a great set on me I am beggard with him he have 8 hens and 2 ducks carried and i badly in want of them
Excuse me for making so stiff
I remain yours truly Mrs Cotter".

Miss Somerville's two periods of Mastership from 1903 to 1908 and from 1912 to 1919 covered twelve seasons with an intervening period of service as Honorary Secretary to an adjacent pack. She loved the wild, uncouth country, where hounds sometimes hunted along the cliffs, or even on occasion out into the sea itself to a small island. The contrast had earlier made a visit to the Quorn a particularly memorable event in her life. The standard of turn-out, the legendary huntsman Tom Firr, hounds and field all more than lived up to expectations and "profoundly impressed the Visitor from Ireland".

Martin enjoyed hunting as much as Edith, whipping-in to the West Carbery and, overcoming her excessive short-sightedness, went very well. Then on 1st November 1898 she had a crashing fall over a small fence when her horse rolled on her. It was two months before she could move her hand, ten years before she hunted again. Whilst no bones were broken, her back was badly damaged. She still longed to hear details of the day's sport: "Tell me about it! Every field, every gap, is of deadly interest to me. I realise them all with sick intensity!" At last, a decade after the fall, she was able to write in a letter: "I have once more pottered forth with the hounds, and have had some real leaps, and tasted the wine of life again."

Hunting was so much a part of life for Somerville and Ross that when Mr. Pinker, their literary agent, came to stay from London, he was persuaded to ride to hounds. Unfortunately he fell off and was not found for some time. His next visit was more successful: "Pinker got the brush," the diary records.

The enthusiasm which greeted *The Irish R.M.* delighted its authors. The girl who slept with two copies, one on each side of her, to ensure she could start reading as soon as she woke, gave them especial pleasure. The war-time inclusion of the R.M. in the broadsheets sent out to soldiers by *The Times* was also a source of joy.

More important in the short term, it earned the authors some much needed money. Throughout their lives, both Somerville and Ross were constantly short of money. The West Carbery supplied the background so helpful to the writing of the R.M. stories, and gave its Master immense pleasure. Unfortunately it was a luxury she could not afford. Subscriptions came nowhere near meeting expenses. As she herself noted: "Have £2.2s.6d. with which to face a frowning world. Haven't enough money to buy stockings but keep hounds. How very Irish!"

Undeterred, in 1912 Miss Somerville resumed the Mastership after a brief interval. In the first season expenditure amounted to £505 against subscription income of £249, though three seasons later she had reduced the shortfall to £100.

One way in which she sought to augment her income was through horse dealing, and at times this proved more successful than literature. Later in her life she established a market for her horses in America, in partnership with an American friend, which lasted until the outbreak of the Second World War.

Edith's world was shattered in 1915. Martin, who seemed in excellent health, suddenly became ill. Three months later she was dead. For many months Edith was in a state of despair. The way in which she eventually found consolation for the loss of her beloved friend and collaborator was unusual.

Many of the Somerville family were deeply involved in spiritualism. Some six months after Martin's death, Edith became convinced that, through a medium, she was in contact with Martin. The conviction fundamentally altered the remaining thirty-three years of Edith's life. Soon Martin was playing almost as active a role as she had done in life. If advice was sought on the health perhaps of one of her adored dogs, it was most reassuring to know that, even if the dog died, Martin was waiting on the Other Side to welcome it, a consolation which grew as so many of Edith's other friends and relations came to the end of their time on earth.

Edith considered their literary collaboration continued, regarding the fifteen books she had published after 1915 as joint works and insisting on her publishers including both names. "I cannot help feeling that I am the person best qualified to give an opinion whether or not it was a work of collaboration", she declared. Even so her sense of humour endured: she was delighted to learn of a poster proclaiming a lecture on spiritualism by a medium friend of hers as, "A lecture on the Road to Immorality with twenty-five years' personal experience".

As late as 1927 *Baily's Hunting Directory* says of the West Carbery that, though they are "not hunting at present, Miss Somerville is not without hopes of the pack being revived". Two years later she went to America, where she hunted, wrote and drew, accompanied by her widowed sister Hildegarde. The tour was a resounding success, almost her only criticism of the country being of bad management of hounds, some of which she described as mangy and half starved.

Miss Somerville's later years were not easy. She showed exceptional courage in refusing to leave Drishane during the Troubles, grieved by repeated thefts of horses but resilient against the threat of infinitely worse possibilities. The award of a Doctorate of

"Miss Guest" from a portrait by Nina Colmore (*By kind permission of Count Guy de Pelet. Photograph by Col. J.S. Mennell.*)

Letters by Trinity College, Dublin, delighted her, and the loyalty and friendship of her devoted groom Mike Hurley enabled her to take a part in the horse world and continue her dealing long after this would otherwise have been impossible. Hurley drove her out in the pony cart on her ninetieth birthday. When she eventually died in 1949, her doctor's hood, her hunting whip and horn and her palette and brushes were placed on the coffin, Mike Hurley blew "Gone Away" over the grave and she was buried next to Martin.

In 1907 another eminent lady Master first took office, when Miss Guest started her Inwood Beagles. She was the daughter of Mr. Merthyr Guest, who was an outstanding Master of the Blackmore Vale from 1884 to 1900. Mr. Guest had run the country in magnificent style entirely at his own expense, always mounting himself, his family and the hunt servants on grey horses, and breeding an exceptional pack of hounds. There were over one hundred couple of hounds in the Charlton kennels at this time, and more than sixty grey horses in the stables.

Miss Guest's mother was born Lady Theodora Grosvenor, and was herself a well-known hunting lady. She was a beautiful horsewoman who went very well to hounds, and was responsible for some improvement in the design of side-saddle pommels. Another innovation for which she can claim part of the credit was the foundation of the Hunt Servants Benefit Society. She was also a remarkably brave woman, once insisting on staying on her horse and hacking the nine miles home to Inwood after a gate had swung on her, breaking her leg.

Miss Guest herself showed a keen interest in hunting from earliest childhood, when she followed hounds in a pony cart accompanied by her governess and numerous terriers. Soon she had her own pack of terriers for rabbiting, descended from Parson Jack Russell's famous terrier Ajax. These dogs bore little resemblance to the modern so-called "Jack Russell", but were mostly long-legged, enabling them to keep up with a horse.

When she acquired the beagles in 1907, she hunted them herself, as she was to do with all her hounds for the next three decades. She and the hunt staff were always mounted with the beagles.

In 1913 she started a pack of buckhounds, whilst retaining the beagles for a further two seasons. She hunted wild roedeer and showed excellent sport, for the deer often made exceptionally long points. There were occasions when she did not reach home until eleven or twelve at night. Many of her hounds went back to her father's old pack, which had been dispersed on his retirement, when the Blackmore Vale Hunt Committee, owing to dissension in the country at the time, refused to accept them as a gift. On the outbreak of the First World War, when the Master of the Blackmore Vale, the future Colonel F.J.B. Wingfield Digby, was away, Miss Guest was asked by the Blackmore Vale Committee to start hunting fox instead of deer to help with the problem of controlling foxes.

After the war, she kept the pack as foxhounds, hunting on her own estate at Inwood and in unwanted, outlying parts of the Blackmore Vale country. The pack remained a private one: no subscriptions were taken though only subscribers to the Blackmore Vale were supposed to come out. A young girl keen to hunt was advised that she should come out for a day. If the Master smiled at her, all was well. If not, she could try once more, but only once. Fields would number around fifty or sixty people. No horsebox was used, horses being sent on the night before hunting for the more distant meets, although hounds had a van. Miss Guest hunted three days a week: her father had hunted six days a week regularly for thirty years. Very much a hound woman, she had little interest in riding across a country, despite hunting in a country renowned for being predominantly grass and the biggest to cross in the West of England. She showed a marked preference for the hilly, unfashionable side, but all the wire was taken down and her own tenants were prohibited by their leases from putting any up. She also arranged for all damage to be repaired and considerable improvements in the way of gates, bridges and woodland rides to be made.

Miss Guest was one of the pioneers of the introduction of Welsh foxhound blood, working in close collaboration with her neighbour Mr. Ikey Bell and with Captain Jack Evans, Master of the Brecon. It was consequently many years before her hounds were admitted to the Stud Book. Like her father, she refused to have the ears of her hounds rounded. Hounds continued until 1954 to be kennelled at Inwood, where their Master spent much time with them.

From the earliest days with the beagles, Miss Guest wore a green coat with a red collar. In the late '20s she reversed this, wearing a red coat with a green collar and green skirt. For many years the entire organisation of the hunt rested on her shoulders: she was Master, huntsman and secretary as well. In 1930 Count Guy de Pelet, the present owner of Inwood, became the Field Master and secretary and in 1936 she gave up hunting hounds herself.

In 1940, following the outbreak of the Second World War, the Blackmore Vale Hunt Committee decided to split their country in two. Miss Guest was asked to hunt the northern part, and her hounds were then known as the Blackmore Vale (Miss Guest's). This arrangement continued until 1954, when the Masters of the southern portion retired and Miss Guest agreed to take on the whole country. In 1959 Count de Pelet joined her in the Mastership for the last year of her life.

Miss Guest had another skill with hounds and terriers. She could paint them most beautifully. A few of her pictures stand comparison with the work of famous sporting artists, and indeed they were much admired by Mr. Lionel Edwards. She had a lifelong interest in farming, being one of the pioneers of the introduction of Holstein cattle into the West Country, and became a founder member of the British Friesian Cattle Society. Numerous greyhounds were kept at Inwood as Miss Guest was keen on coursing and she regularly took her dogs to west country meetings. She was President of the Yeovil and Sherborne Coursing Club for many years.

Miss Guest was well liked by the farming and sporting community. Having been born and brought up in the Blackmore Vale, where she was widely known as "Missy", she had a deep understanding of the way of life there and would help those in need whenever possible. There were remarkably few farms where her hounds were not welcome.

1909 saw the start of a remarkable mastership, which was to become the longest, male or female, in the history of hunting. In that year Miss Betty Dawes, then aged eight, became Master of the Blean Beagles in Kent. Today, more than three-quarters of a century later, as Mrs. McKeever, she is Master of them still. However her part in the hunting world belongs to the period following the First World War, rather than that before it.

In the twelve years leading up to the First World War six women held office as Masters of Foxhounds. During the war that figure doubled. The increasing share of responsibility was proportion-

"The Huntsman and the Lady" by Sir Alfred Munnings *(Copyright: Sir Alfred Munnings Art Museum, Dedham, Essex. Courtesy of Frost and Reed.)*

ately greater than these figures reflect. As in so many other fields, for the first time not only was the way open for women, but the whole burden fell on their shoulders. Whilst a few packs were abandoned "for the duration", most carried on as best they could with large scale reductions. Women throughout Britain from the oldest to the youngest struggled to do what they could for the war effort and to keep hunting alive as well. Young ladies replaced stablemen, the start of a greater trend than those first young ladies can have imagined; women took over poultry funds, secretaryships and whipping-in, masters' wives kept countries going whilst their husbands were serving abroad. Lord Portman, in 1916 in his fifty-ninth season of Mastership, declared his intention of carrying on hunting as well as circumstances permitted, and coming out hunting himself with Lady Portman – as both the whippers-in and second horseman had joined the army – in order to carry on. Despite the struggle, the unprecedented opportunities for some were appreciated. The spirit was well captured by Will H. Ogilvie in his poem "The First Whip, 1915":

"Free Trade" by Finch Mason. 1904. (*Courtesy of Fores Gallery Ltd.*)

*As I wandered home*
*By Hedworth Combe*
*I heard a lone horse whinny,*
*And saw on the hill*
*Stand statue-still*
*At the top of the old oak spinney*
*A rough-haired hack*
*With a girl on his back –*
*And "Hounds!" I said – "for a guinea!"*

*The wind blew chill*
*Over Larchley Hill,*
*And it couldn't have blown much colder;*
*Her nose was blue,*
*And her pigtails two*
*Hung damply over her shoulder;*
*She might have been ten,*
*Or guessing again –*
*She might have been twelve months older.*

*To a tight pink lip*
*She pressed her whip*
*By way of imposing quiet;*
*I bowed my head*
*To the words unsaid,*
*Accepting the lady's fiat,*
*And noted the while*
*Her Belvoir style*
*As she rated a hound for riot.*

*A lean form leapt*
*O'er the fence and crept*
*Through the ditch with his thief's heart quaking,*
*But the face of the maid*
*No hint betrayed*
*That she noticed the brambles shaking,*
*Till she saw him clear*
*Of her one wild fear*
*The chance of his backward breaking.*

*Then dainty and neat*
*She rose in her seat*
*That the better her eyes might follow*
*Where a shadow of brown*
*Over Larchley Down*
*Launched out like a driving swallow;*
*And she quickened his speed*
*Through the bracken and weed*
*With a regular Pytchley holloa.*

*Raging they came*
*Like a torrent of flame –*
*There were nineteen couple and over,*
*And a huntsman grey*
*Who blew them away*
*With the note of a true hound-lover,*
*While his Whip sat back*
*On her rough old hack*
*And called to the last in covert.*

*Then cramming down flat*
*Her quaint little hat,*
*And shaking the old horse together,*
*She was off like a bird,*
*And the last that I heard*
*Was a "For'ard!" that died in the heather*
*As she took up her place*
*At the tail of the chase,*
*Like a ten-season lord of the leather.*

Amongst the new women masters was Mrs. Inge, who took office with the Atherstone in 1914, being joined by one of her daughters a year later. She had hunted since childhood and her husband had been Master between 1891 and 1895, though her immediate predecessor was Norman Loder, immortalised by Siegfried Sassoon as Denis Milden of the Packlestone. The Inge family have given exceptional service to the Atherstone, Miss Inge, another daughter, being Master from 1940 to 1956.

Mrs. Inge, like other early lady masters, was a keen farmer and

"Protection" by Finch Mason. 1904. (*Courtesy of Fores Gallery Ltd.*)

breeder of cattle, sheep and horses. Her Shropshire sheep won in the show ring everywhere, including three successive years at the Royal Show, her shorthorn cattle were much sought after for the export market and she bred some outstanding young horses by a stallion, son of Bend Or, given her by the Duke of Westminster.

Immediately after the war Mrs. Fernie became the first lady to be Master of one of the Shire packs. She succeeded her husband on his death as Master of the pack to which he gave his name. She was joined two seasons later by another lady, Mrs. Faber, whose late husband had been Master of the Tedworth and Pytchley.

By the end of the First World War women had lived down their bad reputation in the hunting field, enough of them having proved their worth in positions of authority. Yet the numbers were not large: whereas in 1903 there were two lady Masters of Foxhounds and seven of Harriers, *Baily's Hunting Directory* for 1921–22 lists seven Masters of Foxhounds, a drop to two of harriers, two of beagles or bassets and one of otterhounds. In addition seven women were secretaries to packs of foxhounds, one to harriers and two to beagles. One was whipping-in as an amateur to foxhounds, three to harriers and three to beagles or bassets. No women at this time are listed as professional hunt servants.

So the principle was established, but the increase in numbers giving women a position in which those in authority were no longer regarded as freaks in the hunting world was yet to come. However the hunting fraternity, often reactionary, was keeping pace with the political scene: the first votes for women did not come until 1918, and universal female suffrage was delayed until 1928.

# CHAPTER SEVEN
# *SIDE SADDLE OR ASTRIDE*

Soon after the First World War, a number of ladies became Masters of Hounds. Several of these new Masterships were to be of remarkable length and achievement. Foremost amongst these ladies was Mrs. Olive Hall, Master of the Carlow Hounds for forty-five years from 1920 to her death in 1965, and known everywhere as "The Miss'us".

Born in 1878 and brought up in County Carlow, she was bred to hunt, her grandfathers Sir David Roche and Mr. Cregoe Colmore having been Masters respectively of the Limerick and the Cotswold Hounds. In 1901 she married and moved to County Kildare. She had two daughters, both of whom subsequently became eminent in the hunting world, Barbara Eustace-Duckett in the Carlow country and "Pug" Alexander there and especially in Limerick. In 1917 Mrs. Hall's husband was killed in the war. She returned to Carlow and became Master of the Carlow Hounds.

The retiring Master, Mr. W.E. Grogan, had hunted hounds since 1904 and continued to do so under Mrs. Hall's Mastership. He was a most knowledgeable hound man, from whom she no doubt learnt much. Mrs. Hall had always had an eye for a hound or dog, winning many prizes with her fox terriers. Her partnership with Grogan was a most successful one, not only in the field but on the flags. When in 1928 Carlow Vera '23 won the Bitch Championship at Peterborough, it was a first for Ireland which has been emulated on just one occasion since. But the most famous hound she ever bred she gave unentered to her close friend, that immortal hound breeder Ikey Bell. He entered the Carlow-born young hound as South and West Wilts. Godfrey '28, one of the outstanding stallion hounds of all time.

Superficially Mrs. Hall was a frightening person, especially to the young. She reacted impatiently to foolish questions and her cutting remarks often made the victims cringe. Yet fierce words to a young farmer questioning hounds' right to cross his land would be followed up by a smiling personal visit bearing a bottle of whiskey. Nor was her charm restricted to Carlow farmers, most of whom gave her unstinting support. All who knew her well were unanimous in their enthusiasm for her kind heart, knowing that, so far from being the battleaxe she liked to appear, she was, as one friend described her, "a darling".

An outstanding horsewoman, she went magnificently across the country. Characteristically, she had her own solution to the controversy beginning to confront hunting women: she rode side saddle in a red coat but without a skirt, declaring, "The . . . thing gets in the way." She had beautiful hands and a perfect seat on a horse. She never gave her horse a sore back and scorned the use of a balance strap. Her main interest outside the hunting field was fishing, which she enjoyed throughout the summer, both at home and travelling to Scotland and Norway for the sport.

Sadly, despite the efforts of her daughters, the Carlow Hounds did not long survive her. Yet perhaps it is a tribute to her remarkable personality: she was irreplaceable.

Even today, women hunting hounds remain an unusual phenomenon. Indeed many people, amongst whom may be numbered lady Masters of long standing, feel that the female voice has not the necessary resonance and tone. Probably the first woman to hunt foxhounds on a regular basis was Miss Dulcie Lambert, who hunted the West Percy Hounds for several seasons in the mid-20s. Miss Lambert had a deep interest in hounds reinforced by considerable experience with them. Her sister, Mrs. Adam Scott, was joint Master of the West Percy with another relation, Major Alex Browne, who carried the horn. Miss Lambert's opportunity arose when Major Browne had to go abroad and, as the kennel huntsman was a very young man, she was asked to step into the gap. The venture proved a great success.

Dulcie Lambert's example was soon followed by Miss Annette

Usher. Her career was a remarkable one for a woman: she was almost a professional Master of Hounds. Coming of a well known Scottish hunting family, she was successively, between 1929 and 1953, Master of the North Northumberland, Ballymacad, Berwickshire and Linlithgow and Stirling, always hunting hounds and never staying more than seven seasons anywhere, and usually less. She was prepared to work hard and turn her hand to anything. During the Second World War Mr. J.N.P. Watson tells us: "After several hours of cleaning kennels, feeding and exercising hounds and horses, she mounted her bicycle and pedalled to Lintlaw Farm, where she destroyed an ailing beast, skinned it, quartered it, buried the offal and transported the fleshy quarters across her handlebars back to Briery Hill, before commencing the evening's routine work."

Amy Fairhurst, who subsequently became Mrs. Simmons, first became a Master in 1921. Her career started with the Tedworth, where she remained three seasons as Master but not hunting hounds, before spending a similar period between 1928 and 1931 with the Quarme Harriers on Exmoor. She then took on the South Herefordshire where she remained, apart from a break between 1951 and 1956, for the next thirty years, breeding hounds with remarkable skill and hunting the bitch pack herself. She was an excellent huntsman and controlled her field as well as any man, whilst maintaining a friendly, welcoming atmosphere in the field. Her other interest, shooting, was also at the time a male preserve. Unfortunately, ill-health later forced her to restrict her activities as she became very crippled.

Another future Master and huntsman established her reputation as a horsewoman at an exceptionally early age. Miss Sylvia Spooner caused astonishment in the west country by winning the show jumping championship, open to any horse, at a number of shows on her pony Joey, who stood just twelve hands two inches.

Any suggestion that this success might owe more to the pony than the rider was refuted, when, at the age of twelve, Miss Spooner started to ride a horse called Sunday. Although Sunday was an outstanding performer, he was regarded as almost unrideable as no-one could hold him. Somehow the young girl established a rapport with him, and they were soon winning show jumping championships everywhere, delighting the crowds with the way they went round a course. Sunday could never resist jumping much bigger than was necessary, especially at a water jump. Over sixteen feet of water he would always clear around thirty-six feet. He would jump whatever his rider pointed him at. On one occasion they cleared a large, open topped motor car, and another time she had the dining-room table laid outside for eight, and seated eight guests around it, then jumped table, china, glasses, chairs – and guests.

Miss Spooner's father was Master of his own pack of harriers in Dartmoor from 1911 to 1925, a pack which had formerly been the Sperling and has now become the Spooner's and West Dartmoor Foxhounds. Miss Spooner had been whipping-in to her father from the age of eight. On her twenty-first birthday, her father transferred the hounds into her name and she hunted them herself from that date. She remained Master for four seasons, from 1925 to 1929. The family then moved to the Taunton Vale country where her father became Master of the Taunton Vale Harriers for one season (1929–30) and Miss Spooner hunted hounds for him. Although he then moved back to his former home country, Miss Spooner remained in Taunton Vale country, hunting for many seasons with the Taunton Vale Fox Hounds.

Miss Spooner fulfilled all her early promise as a horsewoman. She went on to excel as a point-to-point rider, riding in mixed races against men, and on the polo ground as well as in the hunting field and as a show jumper. She was one of the first to make full use of the opportunities newly opened to women by the cross saddle in many different spheres, in addition to carrying the horn with conspicuous success.

If some women were now doing a man's job in the hunting world, others were embarrassing chivalrous male field masters by their undisciplined hard riding. Major Burnaby, Master of the Quorn in the '20s, solved this problem with an effective mode of expression. "Will all those ladies who are either beautiful or virtuous come this way. The others can go where they like," he would remark. Or, eyeing a lady who, not for the first time, was about to jump on a hound, "Can't anyone stop that damned bitch?" adding, very quietly, "I am afraid she is getting in the way of the lady jumping that fence." This was also the time of the popular warning, "Loose horse with a girl on top." According to one estimate, there were twenty-five women hunting in 1922 for every one hunting in 1880.

"The Belvoir Away from Melton Spinney" *l.* to *r.*: Capt. M.O. Roberts M.F.H., H.R.H. The Prince of Wales, H.R.H. The Duke of York, Lady Worsley, Gerald J. Vaughan, The Marchioness of Bute, H.R.H. Prince Henry, Col. George Paynter." by Cuthbert Bradley. 1926. Some Leicestershire fields were less well behaved. (*Courtesy of Fores Gallery Ltd.*)

---

Few can have been more knowledgeable about hunting, the country and natural history than Frances Pitt, who was Master of the Wheatland from 1929 to 1952. Born in Shropshire in 1888, she lived in the same hunting country all her life. The understanding this gave her of local affairs contributed much to her success and popularity as a Master, particularly with the farming community. From childhood she showed a deep interest in the wildlife around her. Keenly observant, she delighted in studying the animals of woodlands, fields and hedgerows as she walked or rode about the country.

She had to show remarkable persistance to enjoy her hunting. Whilst her father hunted, he appears to have given her little encouragement as a child. Rides were rare treats on unsuitable ponies with impossibly uncomfortable side saddles. The only instruction she had came from a succession of horse-minded farm managers. She had constant falls, her first saddle having only a single pommel, and the second being "cocked up in front with a soup plate seat", but at least her elaborately designed and much tested "safety skirt" worked as intended. Yet in time she became a first rate and thoughtful horsewoman, with all the "gumption" required to ride across a country. "Gumption" was a quality she rated highly and showed from childhood: few girls would have persevered against such odds.

In 1921 she became honorary hunt secretary to the Wheatland, before coming in as Master in 1929. In addition to the work entailed in being first joint and then sole Master of the Wheatland, Frances Pitt developed her early interest in natural history. She became an acknowledged expert on animal psychology and behaviour, lecturing on the subject on radio, a Fellow of the Linnean Society and a member of the British Ornithological Union. She showed a remarkable talent for communicating her enthusiasm and knowledge, publishing more than thirty books as well as numerous articles, and writing regularly for the *Evening Standard.* Some of her books are for children, telling of individual wild animals she cared for before allowing them to return to the wild (*Diana My Badger, Toby My Fox-Cub* and others) which continue to delight children today. She was also an excellent photographer of the subjects closest to her heart, and was thus able to illustrate her work. In addition she found time for extensive farming, bred Hereford cattle, sat on the Bench and travelled in many countries, including Scandinavia, Iceland, East Africa and the Congo.

Her understanding of animal behaviour constantly helped her in the hunting field. On one occasion, after a hard riding hunt when most of the field took a wrong turn, forgetting that a beaten fox almost invariably turns downwind, she and one companion found themselves alone with hounds. Satisfied with the way she had ridden a difficult line, she was afterwards disappointed to hear the comment: "Oh, Miss Pitt! She was likely to be there; she's a sort of naturalist, and knows where a fox will go better than he does himself."

Her knowledge and experience were put to practical effect in 1949 when she was asked to serve on the Scott Henderson Committee. This Committee was set up by the Labour government of the time to report on cruelty to wild animals, following several abortive attempts by Members of Parliament to introduce legislation prohibiting hunting and other field sports. Whilst Frances Pitt clearly represented a conservative point of view, the members were selected to reflect all shades of opinion, no doubt in the anticipation that at least some restriction of field sports would be recommended.

The report was finally published in June 1951. An interesting exposition of facts concerning wild animals and field sports, it exposes many of the fallacies credulously accepted by those insufficiently informed. Anyone seriously opposed to hunting would be well advised to study the report and re-examine his own presumptions in the light of its appraisal. Amongst the conclusions reached is one that "foxhunting makes a very important contribution to the control of foxes and involves less cruelty than most other methods of controlling them. It should therefore be allowed to continue."

This is a clear example of depth of understanding of a subject and an ability to communicate it to others overcoming ignorance and prejudice. Some of the credit for this must be given to Frances Pitt.

An equally good ambassador for hunting was Lady Apsley. She also excelled at the art of communication and was even more active in public affairs. Her father, Captain B.C.S. Meeking, was killed in the Boer War, but Mrs. Meeking brought her two daughters up to hunt. Mrs. Meeking later remarried, and Violet's stepfather was Mr. Herbert Johnson, Master of the Hursley. During the First World War Violet served as a V.A.D. at a military hospital, then in 1923 she married Lord Apsley, eldest son of Lord Bathurst. They had two sons and hunted with both the V.W.H. (Bathurst), of which her father-in-law was Master for almost fifty years, and the Beaufort. Lady Apsley looked as well on a horse as she went across a country. Then, tragically, in 1930 her horse put its foot in a rabbit hole, she broke her back and spent the rest of her life in a wheelchair.

Yet despite this tragedy and the death of her husband in action in the Second World War, Lady Apsley crowded a remarkable series of achievements into her life. For a decade (from 1946 to 1956) she was Master of the V.W.H. (Bathurst). On her husband's death she took his seat in Parliament, defeating Jennie Lee in the by-election. Other positions she held included National Chairman of the Women's Section of the British Legion, Director of Western Airways, high rank in the A.T.S., several political appointments and many others. Years after her accident, she listed her recreations

"Lady Apsley at the Cotswold Hunter Trials 1930." From *To Whom the Goddess* by Lady Diana Shedden and Lady Apsley, (*Reproduced by kind permission of the Hon. George Bathurst.*)

---

in *Who's Who* as "hunting, fishing, riding, flying," (in 1930 she became an "A" certificated air pilot) "motoring, tennis and golf".

Lady Apsley wrote four books in her life, one with her husband shortly after their marriage, *The Amateur Settlers*, a hunting anthology called *The Foxhunter's Bedside Book*, an erudite book on horses in past ages called *Bridleways Through History*, and, together with Lady Diana Shedden, her best known work, *To Whom the Goddess*. This book has been loved by hunting women ever since, combining as it does practical advice on horsemanship, horsemastership, dress and behaviour in the hunting field with fascinating historical insights.

The book has a chapter on the relative merits of the side saddle and cross saddle, a much debated question in 1932 when it was published. The authors concluded that riding astride is cheaper and less trouble than riding side saddle. Cross saddle clothes and the saddle itself are less expensive than habits and side saddles, and the cross saddle woman will ride much lighter and can therefore buy a smaller, less expensive horse. She would also avoid the problems with sore backs which are more likely to beset the side saddle mount, particularly if either rider or groom are insufficiently experienced. Other practical advantages include ease in mounting and dismounting, and in exchanging horses with a man. Special pads were used to enable grooms and second horsemen to ride astride on a side-saddle.

The side saddle on the other hand looked better, was more comfortable for many women and enabled many to ride "bigger, better, galloping horses". It also gives a stronger seat: riders of comparable standard will have considerably fewer falls side saddle than astride, a point which surprises those who feel, incorrectly, that the sideways position must be insecure. There is, incidentally, a consequent tendency for women to keep their nerve longer side saddle that astride. However, falls which are incurred side saddle, particularly where the horse falls, are likely to be more serious, for the rider is unlikely to be thrown clear, and the pommels can dig into her.

By the 1930s, the number of women riding each way was similar, with the old-fashioned seat perhaps predominating in the shires and the modern in the provinces. Cross saddle was now accepted, and early pretence at disguise, with divided skirts, had long been abandoned, though dark navy breeches matching the coat were still preferred by many women (and expected in the Pytchley country) rather than the newer trend to fawn breeches. Whilst no-one considered the dangers of a soft hat for informal riding, a bowler was the accepted form of headgear in the hunting field, sometimes with a veil, the velvet cap being reserved as a badge of office for Masters, hunt servants and sometimes secretaries. The cap was also acceptable for farmers and children, but to be deplored on young ladies. A few astride ladies, if wearing the hunt button, wore a top hat. Many side saddle lady masters retained

"Two Busvines and a Cutaway" by Sir Alfred Munnings. (*Copyright: Sir Alfred Munnings Art Museum, Dedham, Essex. Courtesy of Frost and Reed.*)

their top hats, though Frances Pitt was amongst those who regarded her cap as a symbol of Mastership.

The more old fashioned found, or pretended to find, it hard to distinguish the sexes when girls rode astride. There would be frequent admonitions of "Sir, you are apparently unaware it is usual to take your hat off to the Master", or, to a persistent refuser,

"Hi you, Sir or Miss, get out of the light and let me come."

Two particular lady Masters were never mistaken for men but frequently mistaken for each other. Miss May and Miss Violet Wilson were identical twins. They held the Masterships successively of the Woodland Pytchley (1937–45), the Cotswold (1946–48) and the High Peak Harriers (1948–55).

The twins came from a family which has few rivals in its contribution to hunting. Their father, brother and niece, Miss Elsie Wilson, have held the Mastership of the Barlow Hounds successively for a period of more than a century. The twins started hunting away from home, travelling to the Cottesmore by train, and later bought a cottage there. In 1937 they took the Woodland Pytchley Hounds and kept the pack going throughout the difficult years of the war before moving to the Cotswold. After they retired from the Mastership of the High Peak, they returned to the Cottesmore country, living at Brooke Priory.

No joint Masters can have worked more closely together than the twins. Indeed, many people were quite unable to tell to which of the two they were speaking. For they were not only identical in looks but dressed identically throughout their lives. Whilst maintaining a strict division in some directions – a bill for £25 would be paid with a cheque for £12. 10s. 0d. from Miss May and one for the same amount from Miss Violet – they remained the best of friends, rarely silent when together.

They became a well known sight in identical evening dresses at the Horse and Hound Ball, or watching the judging at Peterborough Show. Observers would notice that as one removed a glove or crossed her legs, the other did likewise. To what extent this was done for effect and how far it was purely instinctive could not be told. When one twin broke a leg whilst skating and had to be admitted to hospital, her sister insisted on joining her. They must have overcome all resistance from the hospital, for when they wished to be visited by a favourite hound, the huntsman had no difficulty in obtaining admission. When hounds were parading in the show ring, whether locally or at the White City, they would join the hunt servants in the ring, perhaps rightly regarding themselves as part of the show.

Yet they did have different interests and subtly different personalities to those who knew them well. Miss Violet was a great gardener: she was also responsible for buying the clothes (always in duplicate). Miss May was more concerned with organising the horses, and indeed life in general, being perhaps the more level-headed and practical. She always drove the car. Miss Violet always had the bigger bedroom, the larger share of the garden and expected to be mounted first, privileges in no way disputed by Miss May.

Both enjoyed painting, but Miss May's albums of hunting cartoons are quite outstanding, their wit and charm belying the somewhat prim and austere impression created superficially by the twins in their latter years. Many of the little incidents of the hunting field are brought to life and given point in a way not bettered by professional cartoonists, and amusing incidents superbly com-

"The Misses Wilson" 1954. (*Jim Meads.*)

memorated. A scarecrow stands impervious to a torrent of abuse for heading a fox, a pig sheltering behind a wall gazes up horrified at the horse, ridden by a lady on a side saddle, jumping the wall and him as well, or hounds come dripping red, blue and green from an unscheduled visit to a paint factory, an incident which took place with the Beaufort. Some have clever captions: "Tally Ho Over!" and the rider is over the wall whilst the horse remains on the take-off side, and "Left on the Post" depicts an unsuccessful attempt at using a gatepost as a mounting block. Some are fanciful: hounds lounge comfortably upright in armchairs before the fire.

The High Peak country at least was used to lady masters with personality. Lady Maud Baillie, daughter of the ninth Duke of Devonshire, was Master there from 1922 to 1947, her husband, who like her was very popular in the country, being joint Master with her for the first eight seasons. Captain Baillie (as he then was) hunted hounds. The kennels were kept to a high standard with hounds in superb condition. Lady Maud herself has been described as a formidable judge of hound and horse. Her Mastership continued until 1947, though she moved to Scotland at the beginning of the war, Colonel Stephenson, who had latterly been carrying the horn, joined up, and in 1941 Brigadier Baillie was killed.

Certain packs do seem to have a particularly strong female tradition. Warwickshire in the '30s, for example, prided itself on the way its women rode to hounds and has over the years had several eminent lady Masters, including Miss Beryl Buckmaster and Miss Boultbee-Brooks, whilst Mrs. Arkwright held sway in North Warwickshire for nearly twenty years. The tradition is upheld with the Warwickshire today, when three of the four Masters are women.

Amongst the finest riders of her generation was the most attractive Lady Helena Fitzwilliam, known as "Boodley", who was eventually tragically killed in the hunting field. Daughter of Lord Fitzwilliam, an eminent Master of Hounds, her first husband was Major "Chatty" Hilton-Green, Master of the Cottesmore from 1931 to 1946 and an outstanding amateur huntsman. His wife had an unfailing eye for both horses and hounds, as well as being a beautiful horsewoman. She kept Major Hilton-Green superlatively mounted, buying and schooling his horses as necessary, enabling him to concentrate on hunting hounds.

Her second husband was Lord Daresbury and she proved as

"Lady Daresbury" 1966. (*Jim Meads.*)

brilliant in the Limerick country as she had been in Leicestershire, even hunting hounds herself on occasion. Here she was helped by Miss Meriel Atkinson, honorary second whipper-in from 1950 to 1971, who came originally from the Belvoir country. Miss Atkinson is sadly no longer able to hunt, but she was a great rider across a country and excelled in her handling of hounds, showing particular skill with a bitch and puppies.

The Tipperary Hounds had a distinguished lady Master from 1935 to 1953. Mrs. Silvia Masters hunted hounds herself and held the ladies' point-to-point winners record in Ireland for years. She also ran the Pony Club, and was acknowledged as one of the best women astride of her time.

It was not only in the good riding countries that women were eminent. We have seen that the longest Mastership of all time started in 1909 with the Blean Beagles, and still continues today. In 1909 Betty Dawes was eight years old, but already experienced with both dogs and hounds. Her father kept some eight or nine Clumber spaniels, which she helped to exercise. Her father also had a pack of harriers, which he gave away on going to New Zealand in 1907, but on his return became Master of the Tickham. Around the same time Betty, partly because she could blow a hunting horn, was given a couple of beagles from Miss Guest's Inwood pack and was soon enjoying herself, encouraged by the professional huntsman, hunting in the woods with a bobbery pack. Her father, handicapped in more professional sport by the discovery that he had diabetes and required meals at regular times, was amused by this and established a pack of beagles in her name in 1909. The young Master was allowed to hunt her own hounds on such special occasions as her birthday and the first meet after Christmas, and took an active part in the kennels, as well as always doing her own pony. Already she honoured the hound above the horse, though she was learning fast about both.

When later she hunted hounds herself, she did so mounted. She was an effective horsewoman, making young horses successfully and riding in point-to-points, always side saddle except for a brief, uncomfortable period when her back was damaged and she resorted to a cross saddle. The Blean Beagles were successful in the show ring, winning a championship at Peterborough in 1928. Mrs. McKeever, as Miss Dawes became, later gave up showing and the Blean Beagles are no longer eligible due to a retrospective change in the rules after the use of a stallion hound of hunting grand-parentage but Kennel Club parentage.

The Beagles are a popular feature of this part of Kent, their Master having lived in the same village all her life, leaving it only for six months in America in her late 'teens. They have given many a keen amateur a first chance at hunting or whipping-in to hounds, and many of the boys from King's School Canterbury have enjoyed hunting with them. It was over-keeness of some of the local young entry which eventually stopped Mrs. McKeever from

"Mrs. McKeever with huntsman A. Finn" 1961. (*Jim Meads.*)

hunting hounds herself. Her example of coming out mounted was followed by many youngsters, at first guided and controlled by the Master's mother and another friend. When these two stopped riding, the problem of controlling the young mounted field became impossible.

In recent years, in common with other hunts in the area, the Blean Beagles have suffered at the hands of those opposed to hunting. However such opponents have met their match in Mrs. McKeever, who responds with unfailing humour to their attacks. Vicious and potentially dangerous spraying of hounds and humans with "anti-mate" elicited a letter from the Master to those involved, who claimed some connection with one of the teaching hospitals, querying the precise consequences of the spray and attributing their behaviour to concern over world population figures. She was disappointed in their failure to reply. One opponent of hunting gave such a spirited performance on the hunting horn outside the Horse and Hound Ball that she strove to persuade him to take part in the horn-blowing competition at the Ball. She has, incidentally, a quite undeserved reputation for reaching that function in a van laden with sheep: the back was filled only with hay to keep out the elements, and not with livestock.

When Sir Edward Curre died in 1930 his widow Lady Curre took on his hounds, remaining Master for twenty-six seasons. She continued her late husband's unique breeding system which had produced his remarkable pack of white hounds with their glorious deep cry.

1936 saw the start of two Masterships which were to make a real contribution to hunting. In that year Miss Effie Barker became Master of the Garth. Her father had been Master from 1928 to 1931, she had kept the hunt accounts for some time and was well known in the country. She soon became adept at running the country, devoting endless time and patience to seeing farmers. She was fortunate in having as a huntsman Wyndham Daniels, who first came to the Garth in 1920 and had blooded her in 1922 as a small child. He eased her transition from child to Master and was a tower of strength until his retirement in 1946.

Like many other girls of the time, Miss Barker had no riding instruction, her father simply expecting her to get to hounds as best she might, but experience on a wide range of horses, many of them lent to her, soon made her a workmanlike horsewoman.

Miss Barker recalls that female Masters were still a rare enough breed to feel heavily outnumbered at meetings of the Masters of Foxhounds Association. These meetings were held in a smart London Club where the ladies were ushered into an alcove well secluded by the heads of bison and other trophies. They were not encouraged to speak at the meeting.

During the war, her father joined her in the Mastership to help the hunt through that difficult period, for some of which she was abroad. The problem of feeding hounds and horses was somewhat eased when land at her old home was taken over by American soldiers: the Americans seemed remarkably wasteful of food stuffs and this helped to feed the hounds. These soldiers showed no interest in the sport, unlike the many British soldiers before the war stationed at Aldershot and other bases close by, who had enjoyed their hunting with the Garth.

After the war, the spread of urban development ate away the Garth country until in 1962 it was merged with the South Berks. Miss Barker continued in the Mastership for a further three seasons, but found even the enlarged country was disappearing beneath waves of concrete at an alarming rate. The M4 motorway especially destroyed much of the old Garth country. After the usual teething troubles the amalgamation became a happy one and the country still continues to be hunted two days a week. Miss Barker retired in 1965.

Another, even longer, Mastership started in 1936, when Miss Mary Furness took on the Hurworth Hounds in Yorkshire. She retained that position for thirty-five seasons, retiring in 1971. Miss Furness hunted as a child with the South Durham, moving to the Hurworth country after the First World War. When the then Master Colonel Gordon gave up the Hurworth Hounds in 1936 she was asked to take on the Mastership. After three memorable seasons, war broke out and it was only possible to maintain a nucleus of the pack to control foxes in the country, stopping hunting after Christmas. After the war, Miss Furness was joined in the mastership by her brother for eight seasons, which she found a tremendous help as he knew so many of the farming community well.

Miss Furness soon became deeply interested in the breeding of hounds. She was fortunate in having Ted Littleworth for her huntsman, and received much help from him and his family and also from the Peaker family. When Littleworth retired in 1947 he

"Miss Effie Barker" 1956. (*Jim Meads.*)

was succeeded by his son-in-law Bernard Ward.

Miss Furness is a great adherent to the pure English foxhound, and the Hurworth, together with the Brocklesby, the Buccleugh and the Belvoir, was one of the few hunts to retain the pure English blood. The Master's skill in breeding bore fruit when the Hurworth won the Bitch Championship at the Great Yorkshire

Show.

Miss Furness was eventually forced to give up riding (she had always ridden side saddle) by an arthritic hip. Finding it too difficult to continue in the Mastership when unable to ride, she retired in 1971.

Other long serving lady Masters from the '30s included Mrs. E.M. Vaughan of the Albrighton (1935–52) and Miss R.M. Harrison of the North Staffordshire (1930–48).

The outbreak of the Second World War, like the First, threw an increased burden on women's shoulders. Many packs either had women masters or were in fact run by women on behalf of their menfolk who were away fighting. Amongst these were Lady Ashton of Hyde in the Heythrop, Mrs. Fanshawe (now Lady Dulverton) in the South Oxfordshire, Mrs. Whitehead with the Monmouthshire, Miss Inge and Mrs. Atkins with the two Atherstone packs and several others.

By the outbreak of war there were women hunting hounds and women whipping-in, women secretaries and women working in stables. There were masters whose interests predominantly lay in riding across a country and others whose only concern was with hounds. Some moved from country to country, others never left the district where they were born. In short, women in the hunting establishment were now as diverse in outlook, if not yet as numerous, as men. The only department to remain exclusively male was that of the professional hunt servant. Otherwise women were taking as active a part as men throughout the hunting world.

# CHAPTER EIGHT
# *IN MODERN TIMES*

Those returning to Britain after the Second World War found hunting much changed since 1939. The country had deteriorated, with plough and wire proliferating, where before there had been a sea of grass. No Leicestershire Master would ever again return home scandalized by the sight of a single ploughed field in the day's sport.

Few people could affort the lavish establishments of the '30s. Most private yards had fewer horses in. For the first time girl grooms outnumbered men, and on average each groom was doing more horses than before the war. Standards throughout inevitably dropped. Those on the lowest rungs of the ladder benefited from a less rigid enforcement of discipline. Employers and senior employees alike accepted an increasing share of the work load. George Barker, huntsman of the Quorn from 1929 until 1959, declared, "When I was put on as huntsman, I was asked to hunt hounds four days a week and shoot the other two – and I did." Such days were gone for ever.

The economical, convenient cross saddle was almost universally adopted by women. Those riding side saddle became sufficiently unusual to bring children into the street to stare at "the lady with one leg" riding by.

Many people who would not have contemplated hunting in pre-war days now took it up. A high proportion of the newcomers were women and girls. A few may have started because they thought it "the thing to do": others did so as a natural extension of the love of horses and riding inherent in so many girls. With no family background of horses or hunting, girls whose brothers cared only for motorbikes started to come out with hounds, when indulgent parents bought them a pony. For some it was a passing phase, whilst others continued to hunt for the rest of their lives. Girls of whatever background now had the benefit of being taught to ride well, often through a Pony Club. A few boys also benefited, but they remained a minority.

Hounds have a less widespread appeal than horses. A few women and girls, mostly from hunting families, have a remarkable knowledge and understanding of them. A conspicuous example was Mrs. Molly Gregson, who was Master of the Crawley and Horsham from 1939 to 1961, and was outstandingly successful as a hound breeder. Brought up in the Beaufort country, where she sometimes whipped-in as a child, she had already made enough of a reputation there for the Duke of Beaufort to write to Lord Leconfield in the Crawley and Horsham country when she moved to Sussex on her marriage. Soon she was helping the Master, Lt.-Col. the Hon. Guy Cubitt, with breeding the hounds, hunting five days a week and acting as Master on one of those days. With the outbreak of war, she took on the Mastership, on the understanding that Colonel Cubitt would take back the hounds after the war. Sadly, Colonel Cubitt was too badly wounded to do so.

She kept the pack going during the war, and indeed sport was better then than at any other time, with no shooting and very few motor cars. Many distinguished hunting men from all over England stationed briefly in Sussex managed a few days with hounds. One Leicestershire Master remarked that they were either a wonderful pack of hounds or it was a wonderful scenting country.

They are indeed an outstanding pack, hunting beautifully in the difficult conditions now prevalent in the country. Mrs. Gregson continued to do all the breeding of the hounds for many years. She also helped with the breeding of the Surrey Union Hounds. She continued the breeding policy pursued by Colonel Cubitt, most of the Crawley and Horsham pack going back to his outstanding dog hound Conrad '38. Amongst these Bailiff '75 in particular has been used as a stallion hound by packs throughout England. Cranberry '74 was runner up to the champion at Peterborough and is a very famous line in the kennel for work. Mrs. Gregson's skill received the ultimate accolade in 1983 when Brandon, out of Garland '75 by Heythrop Brimstone '76, won the championship at Peterborough.

Mrs. Gregson never hunted hounds herself but was always well served by her professional hunt servants, huntsmen Charles Denton then Jack Clarke, and her whippers-in. She had a remarkable eye for a country, always contriving somehow to be with hounds. When she was Master she could name the owner of every field in the country, and on her retirement from the Mastership there was nowhere hounds were not welcome. Mrs. Gregson died in 1986.

Whyte-Melville summed up much of the pleasure of hunting in a famous sentence: "I freely admit that the best of my fun I owe it to horse and hound." These words can apply to few more aptly than Betty Gingell, Master of the Cambridgeshire Harriers

"Mrs. Betty Gingell" 1983. (*Jim Meads.*)

since 1942. Both horse and hound, to satisfy her, must approach perfection in looks as well as in performance. She started out with two ambitions. One was to breed and be Master of the finest pack of harriers in the country. The second was to hunt those hounds mounted on horses which had won at the Royal Windsor Horse Show on three separate occasions. Both have been fulfilled.

Betty Marriage, as she was before she married Hugh Gingell and moved to Cambridgeshire, was brought up in the Essex country. Here she learnt to ride superbly and enjoyed her hunting, whilst working hard in between, though the governess did not come on hunting days. She was born with an unfailing eye for the conformation of an animal. Her father was an eminent breeder and judge of Friesian cattle and Shire horses. Her maternal grandfather was a veterinary surgeon.

The Cambridgeshire Harriers before Mrs. Gingell's Mastership alternated between sporting farmers and the short if enthusiastic regimes of undergraduates. The brothers James and John Towler provided a stable background, stepping into any breaches which arose. When John Towler handed on to Mrs. Gingell the four and a half couple of harriers still surviving in 1942, she already had a clear picture in her mind of the type of hound she wished to breed. Hunting the little pack in the early days widened her experience and clarified the strengths and weaknesses of the hounds she was to breed from. After a careful study of harrier packs everywhere, she decided that there were three to which she wished to turn: the Lartington (now defunct but then in the Mastership of Mr. and Mrs. Norman Field), the Clifton Foot and the Windermere.

The success of her breeding policy has been shown, not only in the field, but year after year on the flags at Peterborough. In the thirty-two years from 1955 to 1986 the Cambridgeshire Harriers have won the doghound championship at Peterborough twenty times, the bitch championship seventeen times and the reserve championships seventeen and fourteen times respectively. In eleven of these years the Cambridgeshire Harriers won both championships, and on four occasions they took both championships and both reserve championships.

Outstanding amongst all these champions is Chaplain '73, champion doghound in 1975, who gained as much approbation from the dog world as the hound world when he went to Crufts as a personality. Of the bitches, Countess '64, once champion at Peterborough and twice reserve, is perhaps pre-eminent, closely followed by her daughter Happy '80, champion in 1982. The pack is conspicuous for being as level in kennel as it is out hunting: a well-known harrier judge has said that Mrs. Gingell could go blindfolded into her kennel, bring out any two couple and have a Peterborough entry.

Mrs. Gingell has always hunted hounds herself, showing excellent sport in the arable country where they hunt. Kennels and stables are both at her home at Horningsea Manor under her direct supervision. There can be few more impressive collections of quality hounds and quality horses in a single establishment.

For the horses have been as successful as the hounds in the show ring, and are all expected to go hunting as well. Amongst the best known were Earl Bruce, Parlez-Vous and Badger, all of whom carried her to hounds for many years. She does not breed them, but buys them young and generally unbroken, doing most of the schooling herself. Horningsea is a good home for a horse; the owner of the great show horse His Grand Excellency, realising this, sent him there after he retired from the show ring. The old horse, arguably the greatest show horse of all time, champion at Windsor and Richmond in four successive years and at the White City three times, attended seven opening meets and seven Boxing Day meets with the Cambridgeshire Harriers after his "retirement"!

Few packs can have better relationships with their farmers than the Cambridgeshire Harriers. Mrs. Gingell's husband and son both farm in the country, and her husband does much of the visiting of farmers, leaving her more time to devote to horse and hound. Her husband maintains that the family motto is "Men must work and women must hunt"! So well is the administrative side attended to that all the telephone calls come in discussion before, not in complaints after, the day's hunting.

The well-known point-to-point course at Cottenham belongs to the family and Mrs. Gingell's husband and son have both won races there. Soon, in all probability, the next generation also will do so. For both Mrs. Gingell's two grandsons are showing remarkable proficiency as well as enthusiasm in the saddle and with hounds. If anything will preserve hunting for the future, it is the encouragement given to the young by people as kind, considerate and as knowledgeable as Betty Gingell.

Another Master of Harriers of the same generation to make a valuable contribution to the sport is Lady Lyell. Brought up in the Percy country in Northumberland, she and her sister showed an early innate enthusiasm for hunting remarkable in girls just after the First World War whose parents did not hunt. Perhaps a sympathetic groom helped: she still recalls finding him in tears when the horses were commandeered for the war. Both girls were soon slipping away whenever hounds were close enough, to the intense disapproval of the governess, who was less understanding than Betty Gingell's. Both sisters rode cross saddle and were soon going well to hounds. Then they started to walk hound puppies. The Percy huntsman was not told of the early education of the puppies. One sister would lay a drag of a piece of meat behind her pony, the other would hunt their limited pack, and away the party would go across country.

The future Master did not move to the Aldenham Harriers country in Hertfordshire until shortly before the Second World War, when she hunted with the Bicester and the Whaddon Chase. A forced landing in an aeroplane during the war left her without a knee joint. However she was soon in the saddle again, and, as Lady Farrer, became Joint Master of the Aldenham Harriers in 1952 for four seasons. When she married Sir Maurice Lyell in 1955 they hunted a great deal with the Hertfordshire as well as at home with the Aldenham. The future of the Harriers seemed in doubt in 1958 when Geoffrey Hartop, the Master, decided to retire. The retiring Master's skill on the hunting horn was being demonstrated in a competition at a Pony Club Ball when Sir Maurice turned to him. "If we took on the Harriers would you hunt them?" he asked. Despite reservations in the cold light of morning, the new Masters tested their own intentions by the spin of a coin. Confident from their own reactions that this was what they really wanted, the deal was concluded. Soon Sir Maurice was hunting hounds himself with Lady Lyell as his field master. Following his appointment as a High Court judge, she hunted hounds for ten seasons, until stopped by a broken leg.

Lady Lyell shows great interest in the breeding of horses, with rather less enthusiasm for hounds. Essentially a riding person, she used to ride in the show ring and hunter trials and still enjoys dressage competitions. It is tempting to assume that were she starting today in the same part of England she would be more involved in competitive riding rather than so committed to the hunting world, eventing perhaps, as her daughter is today, although she is adamant that hunting is a necessary part of life for an event horse. Yet at the time the option of hunting in a better riding country was open to her. She preferred to play her part in keeping hunting alive round Redbourn.

This loyalty to hunting has been severely tested in recent years. By an unfortunate chance, the Aldenham Harriers' Boxing Day meet has become a prime target for those opposed to hunting, attracting excessive coverage from the press and television. The common in Redbourn, where hounds have always met on Boxing Day, was given to the Parish Council on condition that sporting activities should continue there. The council then decided to ban hounds from this land. A referendum was held and the inhabitants voted to retain their meet. Lady Lyell feels it is important that hounds should continue to meet there, though the antagonism does little to help the Christmas spirit. That problem at least she must have been glad to put aside on her retirement from the Mastership in 1983.

Few individuals, men or women, have completed thirty-nine years as Master and huntsman and forty-nine years as Hunt Secretary. This is the remarkable record of Lady Waechter, who continues to hold all three positions with the North Ledbury. Her father, Mr. J.F. Twinberrow, together with Sir Edward Curre's brother John Curre, built the North Ledbury Kennels in 1905–6, then Mr. Twinberrow, after a spell as Master of the Teme Valley, resumed the Mastership of the North Ledbury from 1912 to his death in 1931.

Despite his own enthusiasm for hunting, Mr. Twinberrow gave little encouragement to either of his daughters in the early days, bidding them not to interfere. Perhaps he had reason: hogged manes were then fashionable though Mr. Twinberrow did not like them. His oldest daughter, Lady Waechter's senior by ten years, thought otherwise, and, armed with a pair of scissors, slipped into the field where the young horses shortly to be broken were running out. When they came in there was little alternative to hogging them.

The younger daughter Philippa, later Lady Waechter, had equally strong views on the turn-out of her Shetland pony Jackanapes. She longed for him to be clipped like the other horses. She was told why this was impractical but, not satisfied, resolved to achieve the same sleek appearance in a different way. Soon the poor pony stood dripping wet and shivering: his mistress had tipped a bucket of water over him. She was sent to bed for that episode.

Her mother came from London, where she had ridden side saddle in the Row, and discouraged her daughters from spending too much time in the stables. But Philippa's enthusiasm for animals was unabated. She spent much of her childhood pretending to be a horse or wheeling the cats out in a doll's pram. Just one animal frightened her as a young child: a misguided nurse, subsequently dismissed, so terrified her with alarming tales of ferocious foxes that it required considerable courage for her to accept the brush when presented with it. Later she came to love foxes, and is one of the few Masters of Foxhounds to have kept several tame ones in a lifetime, sometimes for as long as twelve years. One fox even slept on her bed, though generally they have had to be tethered on a long chain in the yard. Whilst she does not like killing wild foxes, she appreciates that this is necessary.

All the family grew up with their father's appreciation for hunting. Lady Waechter's brother and a friend even managed to start a pack of hounds in a prisoner-of-war camp during the First World War. When she herself was punished for rudeness by being forbidden to ride to hounds on one occasion, she ran with them all day, to her father's delight. Both daughters whipped-in to him.

After his death, problems arose with the hounds. His widow eventually took the country on herself from 1933 to the outbreak of war, when she resolved that the whole pack must be destroyed, despite substantial offers for them. Lady Waechter was secretary of the dormant country from 1938 to 1948, when her husband Sir d'Arcy Waechter persuaded her to start the pack again, although in the interim a substantial portion of the country had been lost to neighbouring hunts. Much of the country is woodland, with little jumping nowadays.

Lady Waechter was sole Master from 1956 to 1978. She feeds hounds herself, as well as doing some of the flesh collecting and all the breeding. Most of the pack go back to Heythrop Carver '38. She also feeds the horses herself and pulls their manes and tails, achieving the smart turn-out she failed to effect with poor

"Lady Waechter" 1973. (*Jim Meads.*)

Jackanapes. All this is in addition to running her own farm. Farmer, Master, huntsman, secretary and stud groom: each one of these might be regarded as a full-time occupation elsewhere. Lady Waechter has done all these things for thirty-nine seasons now, and is currently the only woman hunting foxhounds mounted in the United Kingdom. Her career is one of conspicuous achievement.

Another lady whose Mastership continues a family tradition is Elsie Wilson, niece of the twins. She has been Master of the Barlow since 1956, devoting her life to keeping up the standard of hunting in this corner of Derbyshire, with all its grass, stone walls and steep hills. Not only have she, her father and grandfather held the Mastership since 1878 (and continuously since 1895), but between 1878 and 1986 there were only four huntsmen or kennel huntsmen. Ted Hill, Miss Wilson's huntsman till his retirement in 1986, came to the Barlow shortly before her father's death and has now been succeeded by his son Chris. During that time, in partnership with the Master, he showed excellent sport and bred and hunted as useful a pack of hounds and yard of horses as can be seen. Both Master and huntsman would go to great lengths to achieve their results, taking several mares right down to the west country for the stallion of their choice. For hounds Miss Wilson has used much College Valley blood with great success. The master is in a remarkably good position for watching individual hounds in the field since she whips-in, and has done so for many years. On any occasion when the huntsman has been laid up, and once for a full season, she has hunted hounds herself.

In the early days of her Mastership she sometimes took hounds long distances to hunt. Countries they visited included the Taunton Vale and Southwold, though now this practice has been abandoned: there is little incentive to leave this most attractive country.

Not far from the Barlow country, Lady Anne Cavendish-Bentinck was Master of the Grove and Rufford from 1952 to 1966 and had her own pack of harriers, the Rufford Forest, for the next twenty years. The Rufford Forest hunted foxes in their woodland country and hares in the open. Lady Anne always had a professional huntsman but has taken a keen interest in hounds for many years.

One of the acknowledged experts on hounds at the present time is a woman who has never been Master of any hounds. She has however done a remarkable amount of hunting with many different packs of hounds and has written extensively on the subject. For many years Daphne Moore ran or bicycled to hounds, at first able to ride only if somebody mounted her, and spent her summers otter hunting. She wrote hunting reports for local newspapers, *The Times*, *The Field*, and *Horse and Hound* and gradually became most knowledgeable on hounds and hound breeding, visiting, reporting on and judging at puppy shows and hound shows. She now lives close to Badminton, giving her the opportunity for close study of the Beaufort Hounds.

Wales has been the home of a number of distinguished lady

Masters. Prominent amongst them is Mrs. Brian Evans, Master of the South Pembrokeshire since 1942 and a most successful hound breeder. On the Herefordshire borders the Honourable Mrs. Oscar Guest was joint Master of the Golden Valley with Mr. Vivian Bishop from 1948 to 1981, putting in valuable work in the country. A farmer herself, her understanding of farming problems stood her in good stead in the struggle to keep the country open and rideable. In Monmouthshire Mrs. Whitehead won the unstinting admiration of that great hunting man "Dalesman", who wrote that she was "hunting hounds and doing it a great deal better than most men could have done. She was first-class and quite the best exponent amongst the many ladies whom I have seen do it so well." Perhaps this tradition contributed to the Monmouthshire's later appointment of the first woman as a professional huntsman, Miss Rachel Green, of whom more later.

Further west, the Gogerddan has been hunted, with occasional interruptions, by the Pryse family since 1600. Sir Lewes Loveden Pryse was Master from 1918, being joined in the Mastership in 1930 by the amateur whipper-in, Miss Marjorie Howells. Miss Howells subsequently married Sir Lewes and has kept the country going since his death. Marjorie, Lady Pryse has hunted hounds herself since 1946. She is also her own kennel huntsman, though the pack has now been reduced to eight and a half couple of hounds. Lady Pryse gave up riding to her hounds some years ago, finding the country too steep for horses, and now hunts them on foot.

The Glamorgan also were hunted most successfully by a lady Master. Lady Boothby was Master from 1951 to 1962. She had been brought up in the country in a strong hunting tradition, for her grandfather Colonel Homfray was Master before the First World War and her father Mr. H.C.R. Homfray took the hounds in 1934. During the Second World War the family dispensed with all professional help and moved hounds to the old harrier kennels at the Homfray home at Penllyn Castle. Anne Homfray, helped by her future sister-in-law Serena Boothby, ran the kennels whilst Mr. Homfray continued to hunt hounds two days a week.

Eventually in 1951 Lady Boothby joined her father in the Mastership and gradually took over hunting hounds. Very knowledgeable about hunting and a good horsewoman, she showed excellent sport. She has a keen sense of humour and is a popular and respected figure in Glamorgan, her direct, outspoken manner making praise from her much valued. She continues to farm in the country, bringing to her farming the same energy, enthusiasm and ability she showed for hunting. After her father died, Lady Boothby was joined for her last season in the Mastership (1961–62) by Mr. A.S. Martyn, who remains Master today, and gave him much encouragement and help at the start of his career in Glamorgan.

Just across the English border from Wales is the Ludlow country, where a mother-and-daughter team ran the country most successfully for twenty-one years. Dorothy, Lady Rouse Boughton and Miss Rouse Boughton were joint masters from 1952 to 1973. Not far away, with the Albrighton, Mrs. J.P. Perry has been Master since 1955.

Another part of Britain to be well served by lady Masters is Norfolk. Lady Cook was Master of the North Norfolk Harriers from 1930 until the War, then Master of her own Sennowe Park Harriers from 1940 till their disbandment in 1979. Mrs. Anthony Gurney has been Master of the North Norfolk since 1960. Miss Sybil Harker showed the way with the Norwich Staghounds for many years and was Master from 1932 to 1944 and 1952 to 1962. In Cambridgeshire, Lady Crossman was Master of the Cambridgeshire Foxhounds from 1960 to 1986. Her father, Mr. D. Crossman, had been Master of the same hounds from 1906 to 1935, her mother was Master from 1935 to 1953 and Lady Crossman's husband (and cousin) was also a Master for three seasons in the 1940s. Lady Crossman has been most successful in breeding an outstanding pack of hounds for the Cambridgeshire as well as being an exceptional Field Master.

As in so many other mattters connected with hunting, Ireland is to the forefront. Mrs. Nancy Connell was a most popular Master of the Meath between 1931 and 1953. From 1929 to 1946 she was also Master of the North Kildare Harriers with Lt.-Col. (as he subsequently became) Joe Dudgeon hunting hounds. Mrs. Connell built kennels for the Harriers at her home at St. Catherine's Park. On Bank Holidays the kennel doors were left open, hounds being allowed to roam at will on her lovely estate running down to the banks of the River Liffey.

Mrs. Connell was always beautifully mounted on quality heavyweight horses on which she really went across a country. She rode side saddle and was quite fearless despite some horrific falls. Full of life and energy, during the war she had often to drive for two and a half hours in the pony cart to reach the meet as she lived some thirty miles from the Meath kennels. When able to use a car, she expected it to perform as well as her horses. Someone once asked her why she always drove a Baby Austin. She replied that they were most convenient for righting when turned over.

Nancy Connell came of a family more artistic than sporting. An ancestor of hers, Nathaniel Hone, had designed the stained glass windows for King's College, Cambridge and her sister Evie Hone followed in his footsteps, one of her best known creations being the big east window at Eton College Chapel. Mrs. Connell's sensitive, capable approach enabled her to give her sister considerable help with the commercial aspect of her work. She was herself a most talented person, being an exceptionally good needlewoman and gardener.

Mrs. Connell had a sad family life, for she and two of her sisters were widowed at an early age in the First World War. Childless herself, she set great store by her only nephew, but in the Second World War he too was killed.

Another well-known character is Lady Cusack-Smith, who, with her husband Sir Dermot, started the Bermingham and North Galway Hounds in 1946. She remained Master until 1984, hunting hounds until 1975 and acting as secretary until 1971. She first hunted hounds at the age of twelve for there was then a pack of harriers at her home at Bermingham House. Before her marriage she was Master of the Galway Blazers from 1939 to 1943.

Two women have recently hunted foxhounds in Ireland. Mrs. Westendarp, formerly Miss Antonia Cattell, has been Master of the Muskerry since 1977 and hunted hounds from 1980 to 1983. She now whips-in and also takes charge of the outstandingly successful hound breeding policy. The Muskerry is one of the few packs of pure-bred English foxhounds, as well as being the oldest pack of hounds in Ireland. With the help of her husband, who is Hunt Secretary, her joint Master, another long-standing lady Master, Mrs. Murphy, who has held office since 1974 and the huntsman, Mrs. Westendarp is responsible for every aspect of hunting in the Muskerry country. Her grandfather and uncle between them were either Master or huntsman or both of these hounds from 1943 to 1973.

Mrs. T.D. Morgan hunted the West Waterford from 1953 to 1984 and was joint Master with her husband for the whole of that time. She was brought up on a farm in the Llangibby country in Monmouthshire, hunting there from the age of five. During the war she whipped-in as well as running her own small dairy farm. She also won many point-to-points around this time.

In 1946 she married Captain Tom Morgan, who was stationed in Germany with the Royal Artillery, taking out with her her favourite race mare and four and a half couple of hounds. Together they founded a regimental pack, the Twenty-Second Light Anti-Aircraft, later known as the Elston. For three seasons Elsie Morgan hunted hounds in Schleswig-Holstein and Westphalia, hunting fox and roebuck. She was also racing in Belgium, where she won two ladies' flat races with an international entry, the Derby des Dames in Brussels and the Grand Prix des Dames d'Ostende, as well as show jumping in the B.A.O.R. team. She has since been most successful in the show jumping world, producing some six international jumpers and jumping for Ireland in two Nations Cups in 1963.

In 1949 her husband left the army and, on the strength of a holiday in Southern Ireland, they settled there, farming, hunting, show jumping and point-to-pointing. When the Master of the West Waterford resigned in 1953, they took on the hounds, building new kennels as the existing ones were too far away. Ikey Bell was living close by in Lismore, old and crippled, but he leapt at the opportunity to breed one more great pack of hounds before he died. When he first saw Mrs. Morgan hunting hounds he was most impressed with her natural ability, resolving, in his words, to breed her a pack "worthy of her talents". He later wrote in the front of his "Huntsman's Note Book" which he presented to her: "After watching you hunting hounds in the field I don't know why I ever had the temerity to write this book."

The pack, as Ikey Bell had predicted, took ten years to reach its zenith. It is very closely bred and many of the hounds go back to College Valley Legion '49, described by Ikey Bell as "*the* best foxhound I ever saw hunt". Another outstanding line has been that of Pytchley Crafty '54, which has been crossed most successfully with the Fell line. The most influential female line was Cumberland Guilty '48. Apart from four more College Valley stallion hounds, no other outside sires were used.

The country lies between the Knockmealdown Mountains and the sea, with the kennels on a ridge between two converging rivers. With no permanent staff, daily road exercise was not practicable. For some years they hunted two days a week in the woods all the year round. Latterly hounds ran free there two days a week, untroubled by main roads or railways. Although there are sheep everywhere, no hound ever betrayed this trust and all returned to the kennels by the late afternoon. The two or three litters bred each year were not sent out to walk but kept at the kennels, learn-

"Mrs. Elsie Morgan on her Seventieth Birthday" 1982.
(*Jim Meads.*)

ing from the old hounds and doing some hunting towards the end of the season.

The majority of Masters can be divided into those who are predominantly houndsmen and women and those who are interested in riding across a country. Mrs. Morgan excels on both sides. Michael MacEwan wrote: "She has an affinity with animals that is uncanny and as a horsewoman par excellence she crosses this country with effortless ease." One day in 1963 when visiting the Black and Tans she left the whole field over eighteen feet of water. She was invited to return next week bringing eight couple of hounds for a joint day. Late in the afternoon they had a four mile point, about eleven miles as hounds ran, in forty-five minutes. Elsie Morgan, the horse she was riding and her hounds were all having their third day that week. The country was big and quite unknown to her. She was alone with hounds when they marked, only five riders finishing the hunt.

Ten years later when her horse shied she caught her foot in a bank and broke her leg. Unaware of the extent of the damage, she continued hunting to the end of the day, even having a fall over some wire, then drove herself and the hounds home. Next day after an X-ray she was put in plaster, but just three weeks later decided to remove the plaster and substitute an elastic bandage. Although unable to jump a fence, she still hunted hounds all day, marking a fox to ground after a good hunt. One week after that they had an eight-mile point, fourteen miles as hounds ran. Only six out of a field of forty-five finished. Mrs. Morgan was in front all the way, having left everyone when she jumped on to the top of a stone gate post six feet high and barricaded on either side with barbed wire. The horse banked it, his four hooves resting briefly on the two foot square stone surface. Mrs. Morgan's Mastership has upheld the finest traditions of hunting in Ireland or Britain.

Whilst no women were hunting foxhounds in Ireland in the 1986–87 season, Lady Waechter and Lady Pryse continued to do so in the United Kingdom. In *Baily's Hunting Directory* for 1986–87 for the United Kingdom and Ireland, male Masters of Foxhounds outnumber female by more than four to one. There were approximately two female hunt secretaries for every three male ones, just two female kennel huntsmen and some eighteen women and girls were whipping-in.

With harriers the proportion for Masters is similar, but amongst secretaries women just exceeded men. Mrs. Gingell was the only woman hunting harriers in England, with about half a dozen whipping-in and as many again in Ireland. The figures for both foxhounds and harriers show an increase in the share of offices held by women over the last two years.

With other packs of hounds (beagles, bassets, staghounds, draghounds, bloodhounds, mink and coypu hounds) only one Master in nine is female, although figures for hunt secretaries are almost equally balanced between the sexes. The low proportion of Masters is because many packs of beagles in particular are associated with predominantly or exclusively masculine institutions, public schools, military establishments and so on. There does not appear to be any reluctance for women and girls to support foot packs: a considerable number whip-in to them and a few hunt them or are kennel huntsmen.

There are a number of husband-and-wife teams, both as Masters and secretaries, with all types of packs. Mr. and Mrs. Fred Donaldson were outstanding in their joint Mastership of the Lanarkshire and Renfrewshire from 1954 to 1979. One family team which has probably never been equalled was that with the East Cornwall where Mr. Bevil Bunt has been sole Master and huntsman since 1976. For two seasons, when the full responsibility for hounds rested with the Bunt family and no professional hunt staff were kept, the Master's four daughters, the Misses Beverley, Colleen, Marcia and Gloria Bunt, were all either whipping-in or kennel huntsman with their younger brother Haviland as reserve for the family team.

Mary Douglas-Pennant, one of the outstanding women Masters since the war, also came from the west country. Her father, Mr. G.P. Williams, was Master of and owned the Four Burrow Hounds. After the First World War, when the country was not hunted, her brother Percival Williams revived the pack in 1922. He remained Master until 1964, when he was succeeded by his son, Mr. John Williams, his joint Master since 1955. Mrs. Douglas-Pennant whipped-in to her brother for seventeen seasons. During the Second World War she ran the family farms, but as her husband was killed she decided to move with her daughter to farm in Devon on her own account. Her farm was close to the Dartmoor kennels.

In 1946 she was asked at very short notice to hunt hounds. She borrowed a red coat from the hunt secretary then sat up all night until she could blow the horn to her own satisfaction. The night was well spent: next day hounds ran from Wrangaton to Dean Wood, a nine-mile point. Mrs. Douglas-Pennant hunted hounds three days a week for the next nine and a half seasons, coming in as Master with the Hon. Mrs. Peek at the start of the next season. From 1949 till her retirement in 1955 she was sole Master. She always did her own milking before and after hunting, though sometimes her cows were milked at unusual times.

Mrs. Douglas-Pennant was a very strong personality, eccentric and individualistic, her slight stammer doing nothing to soften her forthright opinions. Yet she was also held in deep affection by all who knew her, never intimidated the young and was particularly popular with farmers. The excursions she organised each year to the Grand National and Cheltenham became legendary.

She loved Dartmoor and loved watching her hounds work. She got to know the country systematically by walking and riding it, starting with the rivers. Dartmoor is not an easy country in which to hunt hounds, for in the rough moorland there are no coverts as such: hounds are drawing all the time. Mrs. Douglas-Pennant proved herself an exceptional exponent of the art.

Not easily daunted, she once ran a fox to ground in the rocks of Great Mis Tor. No terrier was available, so, divesting herself of coat and spurs, she bade someone hold her horse and crawled some fifty yards into the rocks. A single stone could have started a landslide which would have been fatal, but, undeterred, she succeeded in bolting her fox.

Her whipper-in, Arthur Piper, tragically died following a fall, and it fell to the Master's lot to scatter his ashes over the rocks at Fox Tor, a task which had to be completed at night. Never, she recalled, did the hunting horn sound so loud and clear. Next week hounds ran straight over the Fox Tor rocks. They had not been known to cross those rocks before or since.

When Mrs. Douglas-Pennant first took over the Dartmoor there were few hounds in kennels following the war. She took considerable trouble over acquiring the right hounds to build up the pack, using a lot of Four Burrow blood. Unusually for a woman, she showed hounds herself in the ring in a scarlet coat, her successes at Peterborough, Aldershot and Honiton culminating in the winning of the bitch championship at Peterborough.

"Mrs. Douglas-Pennant" 1954 (*Jim Meads.*)

Amongst those who enjoyed hunting with the Dartmoor during Mrs. Douglas-Pennant's Mastership was a girl who went on to make hunting history by becoming the first female professional huntsman to a pack of foxhounds. Rachel Green was born in Lancashire, where she was given her first pony for her third birthday, an 11.2 hands Exmoor which also pulled a trap as it was wartime. She did not hunt until the family moved to Cambridgeshire when she was ten. An early diary entry records: "Sept. 1st Mon. 1952. First Cubhunting meet at Tetworth at 6 a.m. 8 miles away. Killed one." She hacked as they had no transport.

Mrs. Gingell blooded her that year: they met again on the flags at Peterborough in 1971 when Mrs. Gingell showed the champion bitch and Rachel Green the reserve.

In 1953 the family moved to Devonshire and she takes up the story herself.

"I hunted with the Dart Vale and Haldon, the South Devon and Dartmoor. The Dartmoor were my great love; Mrs. Douglas-Pennant was hunting hounds and Charlie Pengelly was first whip and kennel huntsman. Had great days with them on a 14 h.h. half arab mare who went like the wind over the moor.

"1956. Left school with one O-level and a broken collar bone! No idea of future. Spent some time at home on the eighty-five acre farm helping my father: one week I hunted every day except Sunday (by borrowing my sisters' ponies, they being at school!) On Sunday my father looked over the paper at breakfast and said: 'As there is no hunting today I suppose you might wash up the milking machines this morning, for the first time this week?" This was followed by: 'I think it's time you got a job.'

"The following week we had a great hunt right across the moor and I spent the night with Colonel and Mrs. Godfrey Clarke at Buckland Monachorum. I hacked back the next day to Buckfastleigh. During my absence my mother got me a job with the late Tommy Jarvis in his chasing yard, where I was told I would be well disciplined! I was. I polished brass buckles, raked gravel, cut chaff, squared the muck heap twice daily and occasionally rode exercise on what I considered lunatic horses! Summer saw me jobless again, and then, at a gymkhana with my twin sisters, John Dix offered me a job 'doing' his horses and playing second whip to him hunting the Dartmoor, so I packed my case, gathered up my ex-paratrooper bicycle and my 14 h.h. pony and went to Meavy to earn £2.10s.0d. a week and my keep.

"John Dix's first whip was Sean Higgins who had been with him in Ireland. The following season, 1958–59, John Dix took on the Albrighton Woodland and Sean had to go and do National Service as he could no longer be claimed as a farm worker; I was promoted to First Whip and a scarlet coat! My most memorable faux pas occurred this season. Foxes were very scarce and sport very poor. On this particular day we had drawn blank and it was 3.30 p.m. with little left to draw. John Dix was trying along a scrubby canal bank, when hounds started to feather coming towards me. I was sitting near an old pollarded willow and I had seen pictures of the Berkeley finding foxes up in such trees, so as hounds came to the base of the tree I looked up and hanging down was a fluffy orange 'brush'. 'Tallyho!' shrieks I, up gallops John Dix, I indicate up the tree. The 'brush' has disappeared and been replaced by a large round ginger face which goes 'miaow. . . .'"

Rachel Green went with John Dix to the Isle of Wight in 1959, whipping-in to him there until 1964. She then took a year away and hitch-hiked to India, before whipping-in to the Tiverton for one season. Then:

"1966–67. Went to Sedgefield in North Carolina to whip-in to professional Bayne Walker. Not comparable to English fox-hunting. Hounds had incredible noses, no drive, good music, no discipline. Very wooded country.

"1967–68. Whipped-in to the Montreal (the oldest recorded pack in North America and, as some wit said, 'If you don't believe it, go and see the kennels!') Only hunted from August to December then snowed in until the end of March. No foxes (owing to rabies), hounds rioted on wolves, racoons, cat etc. (Could write a book myself on that season!)

"1968–69. Went to Australia. Only had one day's hunting with the Melbourne Hunt Club. Very wet and scentless, but I did view a fox!

"1969–70. Returned to U.K. in May and was terribly lucky to get the whip's job in August with the South and West Wilts. Bill Lock was hunting hounds and General Matthews, Captain Mann and Mr. Bradley were Masters. A really super country. The vale, the downs and the plain all different and all fun in their own way. I worked in the stables under Tommy Kavanagh who had been there in Ikey Bell's day. Had my first taste of hunting hounds when Bill was laid up for two days. The first was a Saturday. (Huge crowd.) I was petrified. The hounds did not really know me and sat down at the meet and 'sang'. We had a passable day with no great hunt."

From 1970 to 1972 she hunted the Dart Vale and Haldon before moving to Monmouthshire as huntsman for the next four seasons.

For the greater part of one season she was running the kennels entirely single-handed. Her last job was from 1976 to 1979 as first whipper-in and kennel huntsman to the Galway Blazers. She describes this as a "marvellous country to cross. Hardly a strand of wire and all grass. Does not carry a holding scent but they can really fly at times. Hounds when I went there pure English Stud Book and very wild."

Rachel Green is now Mrs. Woolett; she is married to a vet and living in Ireland. Her career in hunt service spanned twenty seasons, for nineteen of which she was in scarlet or green. In those nineteen seasons she only missed one day. She hunted ninety-five horses and hunted with eighty-seven packs of all sorts. One season when she was whipping-in to the Isle of Wight, her two sisters Chloe and Pip were whipping-in to the Dart Vale and Haldon and the Dartmoor respectively (though Pip broke her leg cubhunting and missed the whole season.) She is a great enthusiast:

> "It is the whole complexity of foxhunting that I loved. Handling of hounds, assessing hounds in the field, breeding hounds, wildlife in general, foxes in particular; horses: those that love hounds and hunting, and those that are indifferent to them; getting and keeping them fit and sound. Flesh collecting, puppy show, farming and farmers, the whole countryside, the weather – mostly its effect on scent and farming. Personalities involved in hunting. I could go on and on; yes, it is the whole complex nature of hounds and hunting that I have always enjoyed. The one thing most hunts could do without is committees."

Rachel Green was certainly the right girl to break the last barrier for women in the hunting world. A number of women and girls are now whipping-in, often having started their careers working in hunt stables. Few girls however are likely to become professional huntsmen in the foreseeable future. The job cannot be combined satisfactorily with motherhood, nor easily given up and later resumed, but the opportunity is there for any girl prepared to grasp it.

For many the attractions of a professional career with hounds are counterbalanced by the less attractive side: bringing in flesh and skinning is not a job every woman is prepared to take on. They may prefer to work with horses, whether as an employee, in competitive sport, or schooling or dealing in horses. Other

"Miss Rachel Green with the Monmouthshire Hounds" 1972 (*Jim Meads.*)

equestrian sports today siphon off many of the "horse-loving girls" who might otherwise have gravitated to the hunting field. If a few of these, generally the least successful, use the hunting field inconsiderately as a schooling place or playground for themselves and their horses, numerous others forge a close link between other sports and hunting which benefits both. Many of our leading riders gained a large part of their experience with hounds, and have done much to repay the debt.

"Dalesman" wrote: "Although I have seen many women hunting hounds, and also whipping-in, I do not recollect ever seeing any of them doing either badly, which cannot truthfully be said about us men, for we have all seen sorry mugs making a mess of it." This cannot be extended to include every woman who has ever held a Mastership, yet it is remarkable how many good ones there have been. Perhaps pre-eminent amongst all the lady Masters of Foxhounds in the post war era are two: Mrs. Murray-Smith and Lady Feversham. Both have held their countries together over a long period of time, as well as taking an active part in hunt affairs on a national scale.

Lady Feversham comes from one family with a strong tradition of public service as well as of willing acceptance of responsibility in the hunting world and married into another. She has upheld both traditions in full measure.

She is the daughter of the first Earl of Halifax, Viceroy of India and Foreign Secretary. With the exception of the war years, her father or brother or both were Masters of the Middleton Hounds from 1932 to 1980. Her husband's family have an even longer connection with the Sinnington Hounds, for the first earl hunted a large tract of east Yorkshire in the 19th century, and the second earl was Master until he was killed in the First World War.

Lady Feversham joined her husband in the Mastership of the Sinnington Hounds in 1950, four years after he took office, and continued until 1985, though her husband died in 1963. She came in originally to help her husband in the country, a role she filled superbly for more than three decades, knowing every farmer and fully appreciative of how fortunate the Sinnington is in the calibre of man farming in the country.

Lady Feversham has led a most active life, undertaking many forms of public service in Yorkshire. She has also had published a fascinating collection of hunting ghost stories entitled "*Strange Stories of the Chase*". Although she had to give up riding to hounds a short time before her retirement from the Mastership, hunting remains her predominant interest.

On the death of her brother Lord Halifax, Lady Feversham took on the chairmanship of the hound show at the Great Yorkshire

"The Countess of Feversham" by Raoul Millais (*By kind permission of the Countess of Feversham.*)

Show. In 1980 she received a particular honour: she became the first woman ever to be appointed to the Masters of Foxhounds Association Committee, an appropriate tribute to her unique position in the hunting world.

Mrs. Ulrica Murray Smith was Master of the Quorn Hounds from 1959 to 1985. Brought up in Sussex, she came to Leicestershire for a month's hunting with her father, Colonel Thynne, when she first left school and has hunted there, apart from the war years, ever since. In the early days she would take a cottage with another girl for the season, bringing her horses and her father's groom with her. She later stayed with the then Master, Sir Harold

Nutting, and his wife at Quenby. She gives a superb evocation of Leicestershire in the 1930s in her delightful book *Magic of the Quorn*, the days when an army of second horsemen would parade under the strict control of the huntsman's second horseman, and there was no plough, no wire and virtually no cars, but most people had plenty of horses. In one season she had eighty-five days' hunting on twenty-five different horses.

Ulrica Thynne married Tony Murray Smith before the war, and in 1954 Colonel Murray Smith became Master of the Quorn. Five years later she became his joint Master, though Colonel Murray Smith subsequently moved to the Mastership of his home country, the Fernie.

Mrs. Murray Smith's Mastership of the Quorn from 1959 to 1985 is second in length with these hounds only to that of Hugo Meynell. During her time in office she had seven joint Masters. Frequently the others have lived a long way from Leicestershire, which has thrown a heavy responsibility on to her shoulders. Throughout the last quarter of a century the reputation of the Quorn Hounds has remained undiminished.

Whilst Mrs. Murray Smith has generally left the control of the enormous Monday and Friday fields to her joint Masters, preferring to be Field Master herself on the less fashionable days, she has always gone as well across Leicestershire as any of her hard riding field. One problem which can beset the woman field Master is easy recognition from behind. The male master with his red coat and black velvet cap is easily distinguished: hunting must be one of the few activities in modern western society for which men are dressed more strikingly than women. Mrs. Murray Smith solved the problem for herself with the use of gilt buttons on her dark coat. This solution has now been adopted by other women masters.

Women today have filled every office in the hunting field. Quite as many come out with hounds as men: on weekdays they often form a majority. Many Supporters' Clubs depend almost entirely on them and in most hunts they undertake the organisation of most of the fund raising and social events.

Yet there seems to be some reluctance to accept the overall responsibility. This is a loss to hunting since more women than men in the prime of life today have the necessary time available. Unlike the duties of a professional hunt servant, those of a Master

"Mrs. Ulrica Murray Smith" 1984 (*Jim Meads.*)

or secretary can accord well with the commitments of a family.

So they ride on, these women to whom, in the words of Xenophon, "the Goddess has given this blessing" of loving hunting. In front the Greek maidens run beside their hounds. Queen Anne of Bohemia rides by on the first side saddle to reach Britain. Anne of Bourbon is accompanied by her magnificent stallion hound Souillard. The mediaeval figures are followed by Lady Salisbury and her dwarf foxhounds, and Lady Lade, resplendent in lace, feathers and curls.

Next comes a small group of ladies in long, flowing skirts, conspicuous amongst them Mrs. Shakerley on her lovely chestnut horse, watched approvingly by Nimrod. Disapproval mingles with admiration in their faces as the slender form of Skittles sails over some enormous rails. She is followed unhesitatingly by the beautiful Empress Elizabeth of Austria.

The crowd behind grows larger. One of them carries a horn: Victoria, Countess of Yarborough. The Bentley Harriers pass in full cry, hunted by Mrs. Cheape, her two whippers-in putting on a most professional show, though both are but children. Less disciplined are the West Carbery Hounds, with Edith Somerville and Martin Ross whipping-in. They are followed by another Irish Master: Mrs. Hall, easily recognised in her red coat side saddle without a skirt.

No detail of the surrounding country escapes the next Master, Frances Pitt. Not far from her, two horses approach a fence together, stride for stride. Their riders are indistinguishable: the Wilson twins. Whilst these three are side saddle, many of those around are astride.

Now the crowd is enormous, but some will always stand out. Mrs. Gingell is mounted on a perfect model of a horse, her hounds a picture of what harriers should be.

The cavalcade has no end. Many of the next group will become as eminent as their predecessors in the world of horse and hound. Behind them come the children, hope of the next generation.

For, despite its opponents, despite the erosion of the countryside, such enthusiasm and such knowledge as is represented here must surely prevail. It would be tragic indeed were ours to be the age which sees the end of it all, not giving a holloa and holding up a hat on the skyline for the next generation. It matters not if the huntsman be a man or a woman so long as one is there to cheer hounds on to the line.

# *BIBLIOGRAPHY*

Apsley, Lady: *Bridleways Through History* (Hutchinson, 1936); *The Foxhunter's Bedside Book* (Eyre and Spottiswoode, 1949) (See also Shedden, Lady Diana)
Asquith, Margot: *Autobiography* (2 vols. Thornton Butterworth, 1920–22)
*Baily's Hunting Directory* (Vinton & Co. then J. A. Allen annually)
Beaufort, His Grace the 8th Duke of,: *Hunting* (Longman, 1894)
Biddle, Sheila: *Bolingbroke and Harley* (Allen and Unwin, 1975)
Birch Reynardson, C.T.S.: *Sports and Anecdotes of Bygone Days* (Chapman & Hall, 1887)
Bloodgood, Lida Fleitmann: *The Saddle of Queens* (J. A. Allen, 1959)
Blyth, Henry: *Skittles: The Life and Times of Catherine Walters, the Last Victorian Courtesan* (Hart Davis, 1970)
*British Hunts and Huntsmen* (The Biographical Press, 1908–1911)
"Brooksby" (E. Pennell-Elmhirst): *The Cream of Leicestershire* (George Routledge & Sons, 1883)
Brownlow, Jack: *Melton Mowbray, Queen of the Shires* (Sycamore Press, 1980)
Bryden, H.A.: *Hare Hunting and Harriers* (Grant Richards, 1903)
Buchanan-Jardine, Sir John Bart. M.F.H.: *Hounds of the World* (Methuen, 1937)
Carr, Raymond: *English Fox Hunting* (Weidenfeld & Nicolson, 1976)
"Cecil" (Cornelius Tongue): *Records of the Chase* (Philip Allan, 1854)
Clarke, Mrs. J. Stirling: *The Habit and the Horse* (Day & Son, 1860)
Chenevix Trench, Charles: *A History of Horsemanship* (Doubleday,

1970)
Collis, Maurice: *Somerville and Ross: a Biography* (Faber & Faber, 1968)
de Commynes, Philippe: *Memoirs* (translated by Michael Jones. Penguin Books, 1972)
Conan Doyle, Sir Arthur: *Rodney Stone* (Smith, Elder, 1896)
Corti, Count E.P.: *Elizabeth Empress of Austria* (Thornton Butterwork, 1936)
Costobadie, F. Palliser de: *Annals of the Billesdon Hunt* (Chapman & Hall, London and Clarke & Satchell, Leicester 1914)
*Country Life*
Crankshaw, Edward: *The Fall of the House of Hapsburg* (Longmans, 1963)
Creevey: *The Creevey Papers* (ed. John Gore) (Batsford, 1963)
Dale, T.F.: *Fox Hunting in the Shires* (Grant Richards, 1903)
"Dalesman" (C.N. de Courcy-Parry): *Here Lies My Story* (J. A. Allen, 1964)
Davenport, Henry S.: *Memories at Random: Melton and Harborough* (Heath Cranton, 1926)
Dixon, W. Scarth: *Fox Hunting in the Twentieth Century* (Hurst and Blackett, 1925)
"Druid", The (Henry Hall Dixon): *Silk and Scarlet* (Rogerson & Tuxford, 1859)
Edwards, Lionel: *Sketch Book* (Eyre and Spottiswoode, 1935; *Famous Foxhunters* (Eyre & Spottiswoode, 1928)
Elliott, J.M.K.: *Fifty Years' Foxhunting* (Horace Cox, 1900)
Ellis, C.D.: *Leicestershire and the Quorn Hunt* (Geo. Gibbons, 1951)
Ellis, Maudie: *The Squire of Bentley (Mrs. Cheape)* (William Blackwood, 1926)
*Encyclopaedia Britannica, The* (11th Edition)
Fane, Lady Augusta: *Chit Chat* (Thornton Butterworth, 1926)
Feversham, Countess of: *Strange Stories of the Chase* (Geoffrey Bles, 1972)
*Field, The*
*Foxhounds of Great Britain and Ireland, The* (ed. Sir Humphrey de Trafford) (Walter Southwood, 1906)
Greville, Lady Violet (ed.): *Ladies in the Field* (D. Appleton, New York, 1894)
Haslip, Joan: *The Lonely Empress* (Weidenfeld & Nicolson, 1965)
Hayes, Mrs.: *The Horsewoman* (Thacker, 1893)

Helm, P.J.: *History of Europe 1450–1660* (G. Bell, 1961)
de Jongh, Jane: *Margaret of Austria* (Jonathan Cape, 1954)
*Kelly's Handbook to the Titled, Landed and Official Classes* 1954 Edition (Kelly's Directories Ltd.)
Larisch, Countess Marie: *My Past* (Eveleigh Nash, 1913)
Lewis, Peter: *A Foxhunter's Anthology* (Lovat Dickson, 1934)
Longrigg, Roger: *The English Squire and His Sport* (Michael Joseph, 1977); *The History of Foxhunting* (Macmillan, 1975)
*Macmillan Dictionary of Women's Biography (*ed. Jennifer S. Uglow)
*Masters of Foxhounds Association: Index of Past and Present Masters of Foxhounds* (Masters of Foxhounds Association, 1938)
Montagu, Lady Mary Wortley: *Letters* (new edition Clarendon Press, 1965–7)
Moore, Daphne: *Famous Foxhunters* (Spur Publications, 1978); *In Nimrod's Footsteps* (J. A. Allen, 1974)
Mordaunt, Sir Charles Bt. and the Hon. and Rev. W.R. Verney: *Annals of the Warwickshire Hunt 1795–1895* (Sampson Low, Marston, 1896)
Murray Smith, Ulrica: *Magic of the Quorn* (J. A. Allen, 1980)
"Nimrod" (C.J. Apperley): *Hunting Tours* (1835: reprinted John Lane The Bodley Head, 1926); *Memoirs of the late John Mytton Esq.* (Rudolph Ackermann, 1835)
Ogilvie, Will H.: *The Collected Sporting Verse* (Constable, 1932)
Owen, Margaret Cunliffe: *The Martyrdom of an Empress* (Harper, 1899)
Owen, Rosamund: *The Art of Side Saddle* (Trematon Press, 1984)
Paget, Guy: *Rum 'Uns to Follow* (Country Life, 1934); *Bad 'Uns to Beat* (Collins, 1936); *The Melton Mowbray of John Ferneley* (Edgar Backus, 1931); and Lionel Irvine: *The Flying Parson and Dick Christian* (Edgar Backus, 1934)
Pearl, Cyril: *The Girl with the Swansdown Seat* (Muller, 1955)
Pitt, Frances: *Hounds, Horses and Hunting* (Country Life, 1948); *Toby My Fox-Cub* (Arrowsmith, 1929); *Diana My Badger* (Arrowsmith, 1929)
Plowden, Alison: *Elizabethan England: Life in an Age of Adventure* (Readers Digest, 1982)
Priestley, J.B.: *The Prince of Pleasure and his Regency 1811–1820* (Heinemann, 1969)
Portland, The Duke of, K.G., G.C.V.O.,: *Men, Women and Things* (Faber & Faber, 1937)

Ribblesdale, Lord: *The Queen's Hounds and Stag Hunting Recollections* (Longman's Green, 1897)
Richardson, Mary: *The Life of a Great Sportsman* (Vinton, 1919)
"Sabretache": *A Gentleman and his Hounds* (Eyre & Spottiswoode, 1935)
Scott Henderson: *Report of the Committee on Cruelty to Wild Animals* (H.M.S.O., 1951)
Scott, Sir Walter: *Quentin Durward* (Archibald Constable of Edinburgh and Hurst, Robinson of London, 1823); *Rob Roy* (Archibald Constable of Edinburgh and Longman, Hurst, Rees, Orme and Brown of London, 1817)
Serrell, Alys F.: *With Hound and Terrier in the Field* (William Blackwood, 1904)
Seth-Smith, Michael (ed.): *Steeplechasing and Foxhunting* (New English Library, 1977)
Shedden, Lady Diana and Lady Apsley: *To Whom the Goddess* (Hutchinson, 1932)
Simpson, Charles: *Leicestershire and Its Hunts* (John Lane the Bodley Head, 1926); *The Harborough Country* (John Lane the Bodley Head, 1927)
Somerville and Ross: *The Irish R.M. Complete* (Faber & Faber, 1928); *Wheel Tracks* (Longmans, Green, 1923); *Irish Memories* (Longmans Green, 1918)
Surtees, R.S.: *Mr. Sponge's Sporting Tour* (Bradbury, Agnew, 1853)
Thomson, Col. J. Anstruther: *Eighty Years Reminiscences* (2 vols. Longmans, Green, 1894)
Trollope, Anthony: *Hunting Sketches* (Chapman & Hall, 1865)
Underhill, G.F.: *The Master of Hounds* (Grant Richards, 1903)
Walker, Stella A.: *Sporting Art: England 1700–1900* (Studio Vista 1972)
Watson, J.N.P.: *British and Irish Hunts and Huntsmen Vol. I* (Batsford, 1982)
*Who's Who* 1950 Edition: (A. & C. Black Ltd.)
Williams, Dorian (ed.): *The Horseman's Companion* (Eyre and Spottiswoode, 1967)
Welcome, John: *The Sporting Empress* (Michael Joseph, 1975)
Whyte-Melville, G.J.: *Market Harborough* (Chapman & Hall, 1861; reissued Country Life, 1984; *Kate Coventry* (John W. Parker, 1856)
Willoughby de Broke, Lord: *The Sport of Our Ancestors* (Constable,

1921)
Wilson, "Gumley": *Green Peas at Christmas* (Edward Arnold, 1924)
Wingfield Digby, George: *Devonshire Hunting Tapestries* (H.M.S.O., 1971)

# INDEX